A Complete Treatise
on the
Art of Singing: Part Two

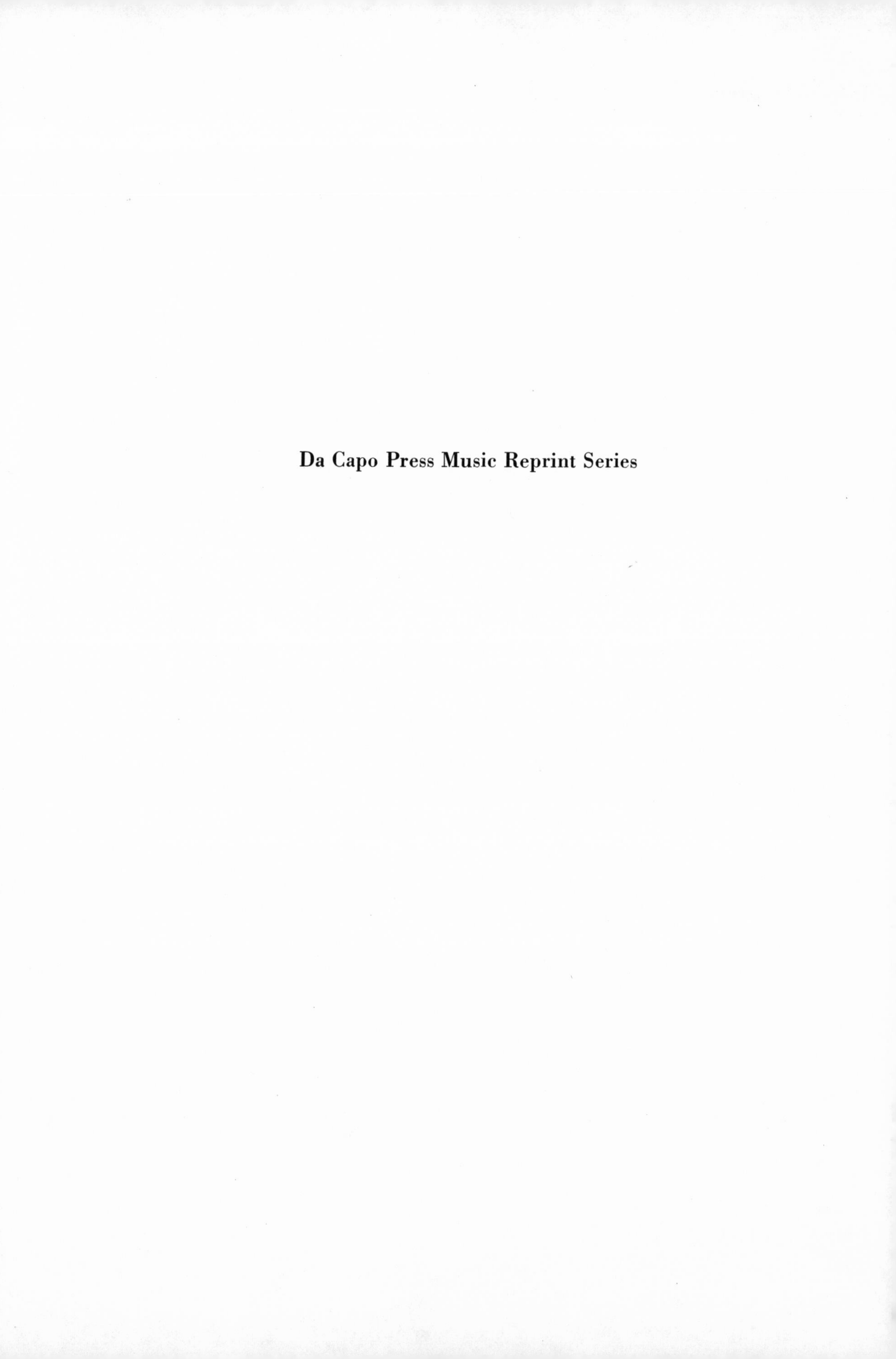

Da Capo Press Music Reprint Series

A Complete Treatise on the Art of Singing: Part Two

by Manuel Garcia II

Second Part, Complete and Unabridged
The Editions of 1847 and 1872
collated, edited and translated by Donald V. Paschke

DA CAPO PRESS • NEW YORK • 1975

Library of Congress Cataloging in Publication Data

Garcia, Manuel, 1805-1906.
A complete treatise on the art of singing.

(Da Capo Press music reprint series)
Reprint of the 1972 ed. published by D. V. Paschke.
Translation of v. 2 of Ecole de Garcia: traité complet de l'art du chant.
Includes bibliographical references.
1. Singing—Methods. I. Paschke, Donald V., tr. II. Title.
MT835.G313 1975 784.9'3 74-23382
ISBN 0-306-70660-1

This Da Capo Press edition of *A Complete Treatise on The Art of Singing: Part Two* is an unabridged republication of the edition published by Donald V. Paschke in 1972. It is reprinted with the permission of the author.

Published by Da Capo Press, Inc.
A Subsidiary of Plenum Publishing Corporation
227 West 17th Street, New York, N.Y. 10011

Manufactured in the United States of America

The School of Garcia

A COMPLETE TREATISE

on

THE ART OF SINGING

by

Manuel Garcia II

Second Part

Complete and Unabridged

The editions of 1847 and 1872

collated, edited and translated by

Donald V. Paschke

TRANSLATOR'S PREFACE

The purposes of this project are: (1) to make available to the vocal profession an English translation of an important work; and (2) to compare and contrast two editions of that work, the latter of which appeared twenty-five years after the first. (a (b

Manuel Garcia is important: first, because of his link to the *bel canto* traditions of Porpora; second, because of the way he combined those traditions with scientific research and with the new style of covered singing introduced into France by the tenor Duprez in 1837; third, because of his profound knowledge of mid-nineteenth century vocal performance practices, a detailed description of which makes up the bulk of Part Two of his method. Last, but certainly not least, he is important because of the consistently high level of artistry and skill attained by his students. It is unlikely that any other teacher of singing has ever produced such an unbroken stream of major singing talents as that which issued from his studio from the time he began teaching in his father's conservatoire in 1829 or 1830 until his death in 1906, interrupted only by two short periods of military service.

The comparison of the two editions is of interest not so much

---

a) An intensive search through catalogues of both publishers and libraries has forced us to conclude that the complete version of Part Two of Garcia's method has never been translated into English.

b) The author states in the preface to the 1872 edition that it is an exact reproduction of the 1856 edition. This would indicate that the revisions were made nine years after the first edition of Part Two appeared.

because of the time lapse and the change of approach to the voice and its development which several years of experience often gives, but rather because of the fact that in the intervening years Garcia had invented the laryngoscope, and was thus the first man able to study the living larynx during the act of phonation. It is apparent from perusing the two editions of the method that the use of the laryngeal mirror in virtually every instance verified the theories which the author had formed earlier as a result of his knowledge of the anatomy of the vocal mechanism and his experience as a teacher.

The author, Manuel Patricio Rodriguez Garcia (1805-1906), was the son of Manuel del Popolo Vicente Rodriguez (1775-1832), a noted Spanish tenor and composer who adopted the name Garcia as a stage name, later making it his legal surname. The father was born and received his first musical training in Seville, and had established himself as a tenor of the top rank in both Spain and France even before going to Naples in 1812 to learn the Porpora method under Giovanni Ansani. Ansani may have studied under Porpora himself, having been in his twentieth year when Porpora died in 1768. Rossini created the role of Count Almaviva in the *Barber of Seville* for the elder Manuel, and the opera was premiered on February 5, 1816. Only a few weeks later the family left Naples to settle again in Paris, from which city they branched out to conquer not only London, but also the New World. After long sojourns in New York City and Mexico City, the troupe returned to France where the elder Garcia soon retired from the stage to devote his full time to teaching. He had already engaged himself in that activity for a number of years, having taught his own wife to sing, as well as his three children. The famous tenor Adolph Nourrit also was his student.

Manuel Patricio was born on March 17, 1805, in Zafra, Spain. He was left in the care of his grandparents in Madrid from the time his parents left for France in late 1807 until they sent for him from Naples in 1814. After his arrival there he was given some occasional informal lessons by his father's teacher, Ansani. Garcia's biographer conjectures that if Ansani indeed had his early lessons from Porpora himself, the later students of the master who lived into the twentieth century could say that their teacher had his early lessons from a man whose teacher was born within two or three years of the birth of Bach and Handel. (c Perhaps no more direct connection to the golden age of *bel canto* exists in our own time than this one, even if Ansani was a second-generation student of Porpora. The bulk of Manuel's lessons, however, were under his father and Zingarelli. Those lessons from his father can safely be assumed to be extensions of the lessons from Ansani.

Manuel's training continued in France, and in late 1825 the family traveled to New York to introduce Italian grand opera to the New World. The younger Manuel's operatic debut as Figaro in *The Barber of Seville* took place in New York on November 29, 1825. The company for that New York season was composed of the father as the *primo tenore*, the mother and Mme Barbieri as the sopranos, Maria Garcia, the seventeen-year-old sister of the author, as the only alto, young Manuel as the

---

c) M. Sterling MacKinlay, *Garcia the Centenarian and His Times* (New York: D. Appleton and Company, 1908), p. 26.

baritone, Giovanni Crivelli, as the *secondo tenore*, d'Angrisani as the *basso cantante*, and Rosich as the *buffo caricato*. The chorus was recruited from choir singers in New York. After a season extending until the end of the following September, the company departed for Mexico City, where the younger Manuel often substituted for his ailing father on the tenor roles. Although the higher passages were revised downward, the high tessituras apparently did irreparable damage to the younger man's voice, and he was obliged to return to France to prepare to go to Naples for further study as his parents still had their hearts set on an operatic career for him.

His sister Maria did not accompany her family's company to Mexico because of her sudden marriage in New York to a French merchant, Francois-Eugene Malibran. After the failure of that marriage Maria arrived in Paris at nearly the same time as Manuel, and for a short time the two resided together while Maria prepared for her Paris opera debut.

When Manuel went to Naples to continue his own studies, he seems to have made some additional mistakes in judgement, such as trying to mimic the huge bass tones of the basso Luigi Lablache, whom he cites in Part Two as the example of some of his subject matter. MacKinlay states that apparently further damage was done to the already weakened voice by such attempts, and when he finally made his Italian debut, the critical reviews confirmed his suspicions that the operatic stage was not for him. (d He returned to Paris to prepare to enter the teaching

---

d) *Ibid.*, p. 90.

profession for which we know he was best fitted.

He began in his father's conservatory as his father's assistant, for by that time his parents had returned from Mexico. But his father's domineering ways did not fit Manuel's spirit at that time, so Manuel left his father's home and employ to enlist in the French army during the invasion of Algeria in 1830. Upon his return from North Africa late that year he was attached to military hospitals where he had the opportunity to study in detáil the anatomy of the vocal mechanism, a knowledge which served as the basis for his theories of phonation and control of the voice.

His first pupil was his sister Maria (1808-1836), who had already made her operatic debut in London before the voyage to New York. Manuel began instructing Maria during the few months when they shared an apartment in Paris before he went to Italy, even before their father died in 1832. However, following their father's death, Manuel became her only source of instruction. She was acknowledged as the unrivaled contralto of her era and became a legend in her own lifetime, in spite of the fact that she died at the young age of twenty-eight of complications following a fall from a horse.

Pauline Garcia (1821-1910), who sang most of her career under her married name of Viardot, was Manuel's younger sister, having been born when he was sixteen. Her father began developing her voice gradually from the time she was four, but since she was only eleven years old when her father died, the guidance of her voice during its all-important maturing years fell to her brother. As was the case with the other members of her family, general musicianship was regarded as being extremely important, and she was given lessons in piano by the young Franz Liszt, and in composition by Reicha. Her voice was not nearly so great as that of her sister Maria, but as Manuel himself was often heard to say, she sang with so much intelligence that her listeners were unaware of the lack of native beauty in the instrument. Her career lasted twenty-five years, and she retired to teach, first in Baden-Baden, where she became a close friend of Brahms, then later in Paris. Like her brother, she had a long teaching career which lasted practically to the time of her death at the age of eighty-nine.

In addition to his two sisters, the list of Manuel's other star pupils would make up much of a "Who's Who in Singing" for the final seven decades of the nineteenth century, as well as the beginning of the twentieth century. He moved from Paris to London in 1848 and taught at the Royal Academy of Music until his retirement in 1895 at the age of ninety. After that he taught at his home until very shortly before his death on July 1, 1906, at the age of 101 years. His most distinguished pupil was undoubtedly Jenny Lind. Among the others were Mathilde Marchesi, who became a very famous teacher in her own right, Julius Stockhausen, one of Germany's greatest singers and teachers, and Sir Charles Santley in England. Richard Wagner sent his neice Johanna to him, and twenty-five years later invited him to train the singers for the first Bayreuth Festival, an honor which Garcia declined because of his heavy schedule in London.

Garcia's first major work as an author seems to have been his

Mémoire sur la voix humaine, sent to the French Academy of Sciences in November, 1840. It was a description of his theories of the formation of the registers and the timbres of the singing voice, as well as of the various applications of them to the different voice classifications. It was reported upon and accepted only after the investigating committee called Garcia in to demonstrate his theories with his students. The *Mémoire* then served as a basis for his *Traité complet sur l'Art du Chant*, Part One of which appeared in 1841. In Part One the author presents the means of developing a vocal instrument which is adequate to perform the music of his day.

In Part Two, which appeared first in 1847, Garcia discusses the interpretation of song, or the application of all the various techniques presented in Part One. The primary reason for selecting this opus for translation is because of the comprehensive view it presents of the vocal performance practices of the mid-nineteenth century, in combination with his very sound scientific approach to the phonation process itself. The fact that it is copiously illustrated with musical examples makes it an especially lucid presentation.

After his invention of the laryngoscope in 1854, Garcia wrote an exposition of his observations with that instrument under the title: *Physiological observations of the human voice*, which was submitted to the Royal Academy in 1855, and was published in their Proceedings. The following year he published his *Nouveau Traité Sommaire sur l'Art du Chant*, which was essentially his original method with most revisions taking the form of omissions rather than alterations. It is a reprint of this 1856 edition, dated 1872 and referred to by Garcia in the preface as the sixth edition of his method, which we have used to compare the earlier and later forms of the method.

In 1894, in order to reply to some attacks on his method, especially his use of the *coup de glotte* as a training device, he published his *Hints on Singing*, with the sole purpose of clarifying some of the questions that had arisen regarding his earlier publications.

Garcia's later writings seem to have been translated into English, but not his earlier ones. We have translated the preface to the 1841 Schott edition of Part One, which contains a lengthy extract from the *Mémoire*. We do not know how much more there was to the *Mémoire*, but we have found no other translation of that work. No English versions of either Part One or Part Two in their first editions (1840-1851) were discovered. However, a nearly complete English text of Part One of the *Nouveau Traité* was published in an unsigned and undated edition by the Oliver Ditson Company. In addition, Albert Garcia (1875-1946), a grandson of the author, published in 1924 *Garcia's Treatise on the Art of Singing*, described as "a compendious method of instruction." (e An examination of a microfilm of this edition revealed that it is a further abridgement of the 1856 version of both parts.

The *Physiological observations on the human voice* was written in English, and was reprinted in the *Laryngoscope* magazine on the occasion

---

e) Manuel Garcia, *Garcia's Treatise on the Art of Singing*, ed. Albert Garcia (London: Leonard and Company, 1924).

of Garcia's hundredth birthday, which happened to coincide with the fiftieth anniversary of its publication. It was immediately translated into French and published in France. The *Hints on Singing* was written in French, but was published in English in two different editions. Both were translated by Garcia's second wife, Beata. The second was edited by Garcia's former student, Hermann Klein. (f (g

In order to make the reader aware of portions of Part Two which do not appear in the later edition, we have enclosed those portions, whether they are regular text material, musical examples, or footnotes, between asterisks. Places where actual differences in wording, placement of paragraphs, different musical examples, etc., occur are marked with capital letters in boxes, and these are explained in the corresponding places in Appendix One.

The footnotes which appear with the text are invariably those of the author. All notes by the translator are gathered in Appendix Two. They are indicated in the text by a beginning of a parenthesis followed by a small letter. In Chapter One when the author is discussing the pronunciation of words as related to singing, as well as in some other places where it seemed appropriate to do so, we have transliterated the French or Italian words of his examples into the commonly accepted

---

f) Manuel Garcia, *Hints on Singing*, tr. Beata Garcia (London: Ascherberg, Hopwood and Crew; New York: E. Schuberth, c. 1894). MacKinlay states that the actual publication date was in early 1895, *op. cit.*, p. 261.

g) Manuel Garcia, *Hints on Singing*, newly ed. and rev. by Hermann Klein (London: Ascherberg, Hopwood and Crew, 1911).

International Phonetic Alphabet symbolization of those pronunciations.

The importance of Garcia's musical examples to the intelligence of the text dictated that we place them in their original relationship to the text, and not in an appendix as several translation projects otherwise similar to this one which we have examined have them placed.

We had to make a decision whether or not to retain the author's references to related portions of Part One, since this project concerns only Part Two. We decided to include them, with the exception of actual page references, because of the fact that we plan to undertake a new translation of Part One. It will include a similar collation of the earlier and later editions since the available English editions of Part One contain only the text of the abridged edition of 1856 or 1872. Similar reasoning led us to retain his references to works by other authors. Some of them are currently available, and others may become available.

Words with more than one possible meaning, whether the multiple meaning is associated with the French word used by Garcia, or the English one used by the translator, are followed by the original French word in parentheses. Thus the reader may form his own conclusions in case some ambiguity may still exist in the English rendering.

The translator wishes to acknowledge the very helpful cooperation of many persons: First, the encouragement and suggestions of his major professor, Dr. Berton Coffin, as well as the other members of his advisory committee. Second, the loan by Edward Foreman of the microfilm of the Library of Congress copies of both Part One and Part Two in the edition of B. Schott's Sons in Mainz, Germany. Third, the use of the copy of the 1872 edition owned by the Norlin Library of the University of Colorado. Fourth, the liberal loan of equipment by the Eastern New Mexico University Library. Fifth, Mike Burns of the Eastern New Mexico University Audio-Visual student staff for printing the photo copies of the final thirty-five pages of musical examples.

Finally, his typist, Helen, who could not have known what was in store for her when she married him some twenty years ago. Because of her constant encouragement, whether it took its pure form or that of prodding, this volume is dedicated to her.

TABLE OF CONTENTS

PART II

PAGE

TRANSLATOR'S PREFACE . . . ii

CHAPTER

I. ARTICULATION IN SINGING . . . 1

1. Vowels . . . 2
2. Consonants . . . 11
   Explosive consonants . . . 12
   Table of consonants distributed by families . . . 13
   Sustained consonants . . . 15
3. Accents . . . 18
4. Quantity (Tonic accent) . . . 19
5. The Stress of the Consonants . . . 21
6. The Breadth or Holding of the Voice on the Words . . . 27
7. The Distribution of the Words under the Notes . . . 32
   Italian Verse (Rules of Poetry) . . . 34
8. Observations . . . 46

II. THE ART OF PHRASING . . . 49

1. The Formation of the Phrase . . . 50
   Various observations . . . 57
2. Breathing . . . 62
3. Time (*de la Mesure*) . . . 69
   Rallentando . . . 72

CHAPTER PAGE

Accelerando 73

The *ad libitum* 73

Tempo rubato 75

4. Dynamics 78

Inflections or accents 78

Syncopation 79

The portamento 82

Messa di voce (sons filés) 86

Tied sounds *(sons liés)* 87

Staccato sounds *(sons piqués)* 87

Detached sounds *(staccati)* 88

Marcato sounds *(sons marqués)* 89

Hammered sounds *(sons martelés)* 90

Dotted notes *(notes pointées)* 90

Dynamics in general *(forte-piano d'ensemble)* 91

5. Beginnings, suspensions, reprises, endings of phrases 100

Beginnings 100

Suspensions and reprises 100

Endings 103

III. ALTERATIONS 106

1. Appoggiaturas 117

Descending appoggiaturas 118

Ascending appoggiaturas 119

Acciaccatura 123

CHAPTER PAGE

Mordent 124

2. Trills 125

The doubled trill 128

The trill mordent 129

3. *Point d'Orgue* 130

IV. EXPRESSION 138

1. The Emotions and the Feelings 139

2. The Analysis 142

Facial expression *(physionomie)* 143

Alterations in the breathing 144

Sighs and sobs 145

Laughter 147

The emotion of the voice 148

The timbres *(metalli della voce)* 151

Alterations in the articulation 163

The movement of the delivery (see *Recitative*, page 177) 165

The raising or lowering of the tones (see *Alterations*, Chapter III) 165

The intensity of the voice 165

3. Unity 165

V. THE VARIOUS STYLES 176

1. Recitatives 177

Spoken recitative 178

CHAPTER PAGE

Accompanied recitative 181

2. Ordinary and Broad Singing *(Canto spianato)* 186

3. Florid Style *(Canto fiorito)* 192

Canto di agilità 194

Canto di maniera 194

Canto di bravura 197

Distinctive *(caractérisés)*, popular songs 199

4. Declamatory Singing 200

Spoken style 201

Examples of Final Cadences 203

Examples of Organ Points for One and Two Voices 208

Interpretive Analyses of Selected Arias 216

Cimarosa: *Sacrifizio d'Abraham*, Scene and Aria for soprano . . 216

Cimarosa: *Matrimonio segreto*, Aria for tenor 224

Crescentini: Aria for mezzo-soprano inserted into *Romeo e Giulietta* by Zingarelli 231

Morlacchi: *Teobaldo ed Isolina*, Aria 238

Rossini: *Semiramide*, Aria for basso 241

APPENDICES 245

Appendix I: Variations in the Edition of 1872 246

Appendix II: Translator's Notes 258

Appendix III: A Chronological Bibliography of Works by Manuel Garcia 260

THE SCHOOL OF GARCIA

Second Part

THE ART OF PHRASING

CHAPTER I[1]

ARTICULATION IN SINGING

In the first part of this work, we have studied the different elements of singing from the point of view of the emission of the voice, of vocalization, and of the mechanism which serves to produce these phenomena. We are going to concern ourselves now with singing itself, that is, with *words united with music*; we shall indicate the choice which one should make among the various procedures of the art in order to impart to each melodic idea the character which is its very own. [A] [Capital letters in boxes refer to the 1872 edition; see Appendix One.]

"The clarity of articulation is, in singing, of the greatest importance. A singer who is not understood puts his listeners to torture, and destroys for them nearly all the effect of the music by obliging them to make continual efforts to grasp the meaning of the words."[2]

*Up to now we have examined the vowels only as means of emitting

---

*[1]Several of the ideas exposed in the first and fourth chapters of this work have already been made public by one of my most distinguished pupils, Mr. Segond, who moreover was careful to recognize the priority of my right. See: *Hygiène du Chanteur*, by L. A. Segond, M.D. of the Medical Faculty of Paris.* [B]

[2]Burja, *Mémoire de l'Académie des sciences, sur le rapport qui existe entre la musique et la déclamation*. Berlin, 1803, p. 34.

the voice; now we are going to see them combined with the consonants. But in examining the two elements of the word (the consonants and the vowels), we will restrict ourselves to considering them in their relationship to singing and from the point of view which is special to us:*

When the singer has not carefully [*avec attention*] analyzed *the mechanism which produces the vowels and the consonants*, his articulation lacks ease and energy, he does not know the secret of keeping in the voice the development and equality which he would obtain in simple vocalization, and he cannot use to his taste the proper timbre for the passion [emotion] which he would express.

We shall present our remarks under the following titles:

Vowels;

Consonants;

Length [*quantité*] of vowels;

Stress [*appui*] of articulation (quantity of consonants);

The breadth of the voice on the words;

Distribution of the words under the notes;

Observations.

1. THE VOWELS

The singing voice is produced by the same group of organs as the spoken voice, and while escaping passes through the same two cavities, the mouth and the nasal fossae.

Of these two cavities, the first is the most important, since its inner surfaces and the organs which it contains are the principal agents of the articulated word. In fact, the tongue, the velum, the muscles which enter into the composition of the vocal tube, the teeth and the lips, combine together or by turns in the articulation of the various elements of the word; the very-variable separation of the jaws plays an equally considerable role in that function. Thus, the mouth, because of the mobility of a portion of its inner surfaces, can modify according to need its diameter, its length, and its interior shape; each of the forms which it assumes becomes a different mold in which the voice receives in its passage a determined sonority. *The vowels are thus the result of the modifications which the tone receives from the vocal tube while traversing it.* "The simple sound which comes out of it," says Charles de Brosses (*Traité de la formation mécanique des langues*, t. I, p. 77, an IX), "represents to the ear the shape in which one has held the tube while pushing the air into it. The differences in the simple sound are like the differences in that shape; from which it follows that they are infinite, since a flexible tube can be guided through imperceptible gradations, from its largest diameter and its greatest length to its most contracted and most shortened shape." *As a consequence, the number of the vowels must necessarily depend upon the structure and the mobility of the organs; also one sees this number determined in a very variable manner according to the different authors.*

For the French language, it has been successively raised, by the various grammarians, from seven to seventeen.

The Italians ordinarily recognize only seven vowels: [a], [e], [ɛ], [i], [o], [ɔ], [u]. One could however admit ten or more of them, for each of these five vowels has at least two timbres. [C]

The experience of languages fully justifies the assertion of de Brosses, and demonstrates that the number of the vowels, or, if one wishes, of the nuances of the vowels, is unlimited. In fact, although writing represents the vowels by invariable symbols, each of them offers us some easily recognized differences when we hear them emitted by various individuals. Moreover, the same person, pronouncing the same word, does not always give the vowels in it the same sonority and value. As soon as any emotion moves the person speaking, the vowels undergo the involuntary influence of that emotion and strike our ears by their clearer or more covered nuance, by their more brilliant or more sombre timbre. For the word *amour*, for example, the [a] will not keep the same nuance [or shade] in a movement of tenderness and in anger, in joking, prayer, or threat. Each vowel, although it may receive a multitude of modifications, does not appear to undergo any of them, and is constantly represented with an invariable type. It is easy to explain this illusion; in the utterance of a thought, all the vowels are found altered in the same proportion, their relationship remains the same; only their aggregate has taken a tint in accord with the special emotion which the one speaking or singing is expressing.

*Two principal mechanisms give birth to all the variety of the *pure vowels*. The first rests on the alteration of the length and diameter which the vocal tube takes on in proportion to the movement of the larynx and the pharynx. It has been spoken of in detail in the clear and sombre timbres (*Mémoire sur la voix humaine*). These movements suffice to produce a first series of vowels included between [a] and [ɔ]. The gradual bringing together of the lips closes the timbre of the [ɔ], and then changes it into [u]. The second mechanism consists of the modifications which the vocal tube receives in proportion to the movements of the tongue. That organ applies its edges in various manners against the teeth, and the [a] being taken as a point of departure, there results from that action a series of vowels included between [a] and [e], [e] and [i]. These two latter will be converted into [ø] and [y], if to the proper placement of the organs for producing each of them one adds the bringing together of the lips.*

*The *impure vowels* like the gutteral Russian L, the French nasals, etc., require the action of the base of the tongue or of the velum in order to be formed.[3]*

In bringing together that which precedes with what we have said of the mechanism of the timbres, one will recognize between the production of the vowels and that of the timbres a straight analogy. From this relationship of mechanism results necessarily a relationship of mutual dependence between vowel and timbre: one would not be able to modify one without modifying the other. This observation is fertile in results for the singer. It will serve him *to determine in the use of each*

---

*[3]The special facts relative to the principle which we have just exposed are perfectly observed and described by M. Urbain Gentelet de Lyon, in his work entitled: *Essai pratique sur le mécanism de la prononciation*.*

vowel the timbre most appropriate to the effect which he intends, and will permit him *to maintain at the same time a perfect equality throughout the entire compass of the voice.* In fact, the choice of the timbre for each vowel is dependent upon two different things: the logical or declamatory accent, and the need to maintain in the instrument an irreproachable equality and purity throughout all its range. Some examples seem necessary in order to clarify our thought.

1. The timbre of the voice should be modified as much as our emotions require.

If the melody and the words express a profound sadness, the timbre which would make the instrument sparkle would falsify the thought. For example, the bursting tone which is appropriate to the entry of Figaro:

"Largo al factotum della città,"

or the aria of Don Giovanni:

"Fin ch'han dal vino,"

would be squalling and out of place in the aria of Edgard:

"Fra poco a me ricovero,"

or in the andante from *William Tell:*

"Sois immobile et vers la terre." [D]

If the melody, on the contrary, expresses brilliant sentiments, the clear timbre can furnish both the color of the emotion, and the ringing emission of the sound. The covered timbre would produce the effect of hoarseness.

2. But, while modifying the timbres of the voice as much as the

emotion requires, it is necessary to maintain a perfect equality in all the tones; and to that occasion, we will lay down an important rule.

In order that the ear may determine the equality of the voice, the singer, by a skillful manipulation [*jeu*] of the phonatory organs, should modify the vowel almost imperceptibly. He should round it moderately and by progressive nuances for the high tones. Likewise, for the low tones he will clarify it, in such a manner that the apparent equality of the voice is produced by a real, but well managed, inequality of the vowel.[4] This procedure, applied to the various vowels, furnishes us with the following table:

[a] approaches [ɔ];

---

[4]*In order to perfect that equality so necessary among all the tones of the voice, we advise maintaining always the same separation between the jaws for all the vowels without exception. That separation should not be exaggerated, cumbersome or awkward; in order to obtain it in an exact amount, the student will let the lower jaw fall by itself, and as it were, by its own weight.*

A common fault among students is a certain stiffness in the action of the lifting muscles of the jaw. It is sufficient, in order to make it disappear, to place laterally between the jaws a little piece of wood or cork; one can also place on the chin, immediately below the lower lip, a ribbon, of which the ends are tied behing the neck, and one then practices pronouncing all the vowels with the least effort possible.

The vowels are produced exclusively by the glottis and the buccal canal, that is, the space included between the larynx and the base of the tongue and the velum. It is the same with the timbres. The anterior part of the buccal cavity and the labial opening have no other function than to permit the exit of the tones. In fact, the Italian [a], [ɛ], and [e], and in general all the open and rounded vowels should be produced without the participation of the lips. The narrow and dark vowels like the [o], [ø], [u] and [y] are the only ones which want the lips brought together. These procedures, at the same time as they favor the emission of the voice and add ease and clarity of articulation, prevent those abrupt transitions from one timbre to the other which resemble the barking of a dog.

[ε] approaches [e], then [ø];

[i] approaches [y] without the help of the lips;

[o] approaches [u]. (a

The application of this precept includes each register in its entirety.[5] If the vowel remained constantly open like the "A" in *armée*, for example, it would communicate the brilliance of the low and middle tones fully, but the higher notes would be shrill. On the contrary, the vowel which would be invariably covered, like the "O" in *apôtre*, would give the high notes a full and rounded color, while it would make the low tones dull and muted.

Each vowel, when it is clarified, follows a pattern opposite to that indicated in the table above. For example, [u] approaches [o], [ɔ] approaches [a], etc. (b

Let us note again that the too-shrill vowels, like the Italian [u] and [i], and the French [y], tighten the organ and obstruct it in all parts. In order to avoid this inconvenience, the singer will take care to open these vowels a little more than spoken pronunciation allows.

The various alterations of the vowels with which we are concerned should always be governed by a refined taste; their use must be justified by an incontestable necessity: here only experience can serve as a guide. The need to master all the colors of the voice has caused

---

*[5]Notice that we are considering here the falsetto and head registers as making only one. (See *Physiology*, Part I.)*

us to improvise the following exercise; we consider it one of the most useful which our experience has suggested to us. *On a single note and with a single breath, pass gradually through all the timbres from the most clear to the most sombre, and then with another breath pass from the sombre timbre to the clear timbre.*[6] The sound must keep a uniform degree of force during the whole operation. This study is really effective only in the chest register and between the tones *a* and $f\#^1$; aided by the exercise which unifies the registers, it teaches the mastery of all the movements of the throat and the production at will of all the sounds of diverse natures.

We have seen that the emission of the voice is operated by two tubes. The second of these tubes is the nose. Its function is to contribute to the sonority of the voice when the mouth is open, and to completely modify the sounds in their transmission with a nasal resonance when the mouth is closed, whether by the tongue for [n], or by the lips for [m].

---

[6] In order to work appropriately, the student will recall (see Part One) that the clear timbre results from a mechanism diametrically opposed to that of the sombre timbre, and that each timbre is formed by the double action, exerted in opposite directions, of the larynx and the velum. For the clear timbre, these two members are drawn toward each other, they contract and shorten the pharynx. In this position, the voice first takes on a brilliancy, then becomes thin and squalling, and is finally extinguished by the closure of the glottis. The movement of deglutition can serve to make us understand this procedure. For the sombre timbre, on the other hand, the velum is lifted, and the larynx, by lowering, elongates and enlarges the pharynx. The exaggeration of these movements produces such a separation of the vocal cords that they can no longer produce anything but a muted noise. One will observe that the immoderate use of these two contrary procedures leads to the same result: the extinguishing of the voice.

The Italians do not have any vowels properly called "nasal"; with them, the nose communicates its resonance only in the [m] and the [n], when one of these consonants begins or ends a syllable, but never during the duration of the vowel. Examples:

[a...n dʒe lo; tɛ...m po; n...ɛ...m bo; m...a...n to.]

[E] The nasals, [m] and [n], in the French language take two different resonances and are produced by two very distinct means. The first resonance, identical in every detail to that of the Italian consonants, is heard when the [m] and [n] are found placed before vowels: *mégère*, [meʒɛr], *néron* [nerɔ̃]; the second, more thick, if I dare say so, is recognized when the same consonants follow the vowels, and forms the real resonance of the nasal vowels: *temps* [tɑ̃], *Rhin* [rɛ̃]. Neither the tongue nor the lips have any immediate part in this resonance; it is uniquely due to the direction which the column of sound takes with reference to the velum. When this organ is placed in the middle of the column of sound, it divides it into two currents, which escape, one through the nostrils, the other through the mouth. The noise which is thus produced fulfils indistinctly the functions of the [m] or the [n].

In French singing [of Italian] one can often hear the nasal reverberation, not only after the vowel, but even while it is being produced. This regular method of the delivery and of the declamation seems to us incompatible with the pleasantness of the singing voice, and we dare all the more freely to reject it, since it has already been forbidden by some French musicians and grammarians. We shall cite, among others, some authorities who seem to us unimpeachable: Brossard,[7] Bérard,[8] de Brosses.[9] [E]

The vowels should always be attacked by the coup de glotte, *and with the degree of force which is appropriate to the phrase.* One should scrupulously avoid having them preceded by the *aspiration*, the symbol for which is [h]. The use of the aspiration will be reserved for sighs, etc. (see the article on Expression); its use in every other circumstance distorts the meaning [*sens*] of the words, or produces the faults which we have discussed in the first part.

2. THE CONSONANTS

The consonants are produced by two different operations of the organs of articulation. They are born either: (1) from the pressure of two parts of the instrument against each other, and from the *explosion* of air which one hears at the moment when these two parts are separated; or (2) from the *incomplete* and variable *approximation* of these same

---

[7]It is necessary first to pronounce the vowel purely and simply, to continue the same sound during the entire passage, and to give only on the last note, or at the end of that passage, that touch [*coup*] of the nose which makes the [m] or the [n] heard.

*Brossard, *Dictionnaire de Musique*, 1703. Treatise on the manner of pronouncing words well in Italian, etc., by the letter "A." One can say, more physiologically, that one should disrupt the column of air by lowering the velum only at the moment of leaving the vowel, and not while one is forming it. It is useless to add that if the vowel has only an instant of duration, the two operations will need to be united into a single one.*

*[8]*L'Art du chant*, pp. 85-86.*

*[9]*Traité de la formation mécanique des langues*, pp. 146-147.*

organs, and from the various continuing noises which the disturbed air creates during its emission.[10]

From these two procedures result the classification of the consonants into *explosive* and *sustained*, a division which is of the highest importance in singing.[11]

Explosive Consonants

These consonants, and this is their distinct characteristic, do not make any noise before the explosion which makes them heard. In order to form them, the organs are first put in contact in an absolute manner, and after some moments of pressure, they are separated, and the consonant is caused to be heard. These two contrary and indispensable movements are named, the first, the *preparation*, the second, the

---

*[10]The first of these principles belongs to Court de Gébelin (*Histoire Naturelle de la parole*, Paris, Chapter 10, p. 85); I have made it the basis of my work.*

[11]The organs of articulation are combined in pairs, and this operation is effected by five principal manners:

The lips are combined with each other: [p] and [m];
The upper teeth with the lower lip: [f] and [v];
The end of the tongue with the teeth: [t] and [d];
The forward part of the tongue with the palate: [n] and [l];
The base of the tongue with the palatal arch: [k] and [g].

Each system of organs can thus form only one consonant; one can indeed assure that there are no *pure* explosives in an idiom of only five consonants, always the same, and serving, so to say, as a type for all the others.

Each of the above enumerated combinations gives birth to a different family of consonants, and these families together offer the total of consonants in use. In the table which follows, I have distributed by families the consonants which are known to me, grouping them according to the names of the organs which serve to produce them, and according to their explosive or sustained character. [F]

explosion of the consonant. From this procedure are born the sounds [p], [f], [t], [tʃ], [k]. During the preparation, the air is cut off and amassed. The explosion which follows is as much louder as the preparation was longer, and the obstacle opposing the air more complete. This effect is analogous to that of the *coup de glotte* for the attacking of tones.

One counts among the explosives the letters [b], [d], [g]; every time the explosion is preceded by a light resonant sound which lasts the very short time that the mouth or pharynx are being filled with air, the first cavity for the [b] and [d], the second for the [g]. Without this sound, these three letters would be confused with the three corresponding explosives, [p], [t], [k].

Family	Consonant	Description
1st Family - Labials.	Explosive [p] pure	Complete approximation, silent preparation, explosion.
	Explosive [b] mixed	Complete approximation, light preparatory sound, explosion.
	Sustained [m]	Complete approximation, sustained nasal sound, explosion.
2nd Family - Labio-dentals.	Explosive [f] pure	Complete approximation, silent preparation, explosion. The [f] can be aligned with the explosives or with the sustained, according to the energy deployed in the articulation. The first characteristic, which is also the most straightforward, serves to complete the classification of the five families: I preferred it.

Family	Consonant	Description
2nd Family - Labio-dentals (continued).	Sustained [v]	Incomplete approximation, hissingly sustained. The [v] can be, at the pleasure of the one articulating it, either a mixed explosive, or sustained. I have preferred the second of these two characteristics.
3rd Family - Linguo-dentals.	Explosive [t] pure	Complete approximation, silent preparation, explosion.
	Explosive [d] mixed	Complete approximation, light preparatory sound, explosion.
	Sustained English TH, Spanish C (*cena*), Z [θ]	Incomplete approximation, hissingly [*sifflement*] sustained.
4th Family - Linguo-palatals.	Explosive Italian C (*ciò*) [tʃ], pure	Complete approximation, silent preparation, explosion.
	Sustained [l], [ʎ], [n], [ɲ], mixed	Complete approximation, preparation sustained with various nuances, explosion.
	Sustained [r]	Sustained vibration of the tip of the tongue.
	Sustained [ʒ], [ʃ], [gz], [s], [z]	Incomplete approximation, hissing sounds of various natures.
5th Family - Linguo-gutterals.	Explosive hard C, K, Q [k], pure	Complete approximation, silent preparation, explosion.
	Explosive hard [g], mixed	Complete approximation, light preparatory sound, explosion.
	Sustained Spanish J, vibration of the uvula, gutteral Russian L	Incomplete approximation, sustained sounds of different natures.

Resume: 5 pure explosives - [p], [f], [t], [tʃ], [k],
silent preparation, explosion.
3 mixed explosives - [b], [d], [g],
light preparatory sound, explosion.
5 sustained - [m], [n], [ɲ], [l], [ʎ],
sustained preparation, explosion.

Sustained - [r], [ɵ], [ð], [ʃ], [gz], [s], [z], [v],
sustained tone or fricative [*bruit ou sifflement continu*]. G

Sustained Consonants

These consonants produce a friction [*sifflement*] which one can prolong at will; for example: [ʃ], [gz], [s]; or else they cause a prolonged sound like the letters [m], [n], [ɲ], [l], [ʎ]. The first are born of the partial approximation of the organs, operating by diverse means which we will not try to describe; the second require that the same organs be placed in a perfect contact. This contact could not cease without producing a kind of explosion. It follows that the consonants with which we are now concerned, as well as those called explosives, have their preparation and their explosion. The sound which they make can be easily changed into a musical tone. Thus transformed, this sound permits the voice to be prolonged from one syllable to the one following, and the singing gains from it much breadth. F

The pupil should learn exactly the points at which these organs are placed in contact, and the mode of action which serves to form each consonant. *Thus prepared, he will know how to limit these movements to only the indispensable organs, and to restrain these to the simplest and most natural action.*

For lack of having given to this study the care which it

requires, some singers add to the necessary movements the action of useless organs, and for example, put the lips or the jaw to work when only the tongue should act.

Others produce the consonants by a badly controlled mechanism; they take the stress at a point too extended, or displace the point of contact as in the affected [d] and [t]. Examples:

Contento [kontɛnəto] for [kontɛnto],
Tempo [tɛməpo] for [tɛmpo],
Tanti [dandi] for [tanti], [H]
Calma [kaləma] for [kalma],
Dunque [dunəkwe] for [duŋkwe],
Giorno [dʒorəno] for [dʒorno].

Others adopt the hard movements of the organs, whereas they ought to use the soft movements. Examples:

Sarò [sar:rɔ] for [sarɔ],
Farò [far:rɔ] for [farɔ],
Il core [il kɔr:re] for [il kɔre],
Abbandona [ab:bandon:na] for [ab:bandona],
Crudele [krudɛl:le] for [krudɛle].

Jamais [ʃamɛ] for [ʒamɛ],
Généreux [ʃenerø] for [ʒenerø].

Others, whose syllabication is too weak, say, for example:

Bello [bɛlo] for [bɛl:lo],
Alla donna [ala dɔna] for [al:la dɔn:na],
Amplesso [amplɛso] for [amplɛs:so],
Sempre [sɛmbre] for [sɛmpre].[12] [I]

---

*[12]Here is a list of faults extracted from *L'Art du chant* by Bérard, p. 52. Since him, it has diminished slightly [*faiblement*]:

Armide [arəmidə] for [armidə],
Brûler [bəryle] for [bryle],
J'adore [ʃadɔr] for [ʒadɔr],
Jardin [ʃardɛ̃] for [ʒardɛ̃],
Géant [ʃeã] for [ʒeã],
Il est [il hɛ] for [ilɛ],

Others have the fault of overly exaggerating the trilled [r], or of lisping.

Others, finally, chew their words, or pronounce them between their teeth in such a manner as to render themselves unintelligible.[13]

[J] In order to train the organs, to develop all their force, or to overcome their habitual softness, it is necessary to endeavor to join to each syllable the consonants of the following syllable, and to make the encroachment heard in the pronunciation. In this manner, *the vowels will always be found to begin the syllable, and the consonants to finish it.*[14]

Examples:

Deh parlate che forse tacendo
[dep arl at ek ef ɔrs et atʃ ɛnd o]
Men pietosi, piu barbari siete, etc.
[menp iet oz ip iub arb ar is iet e].
(Aria by Cimarosa in *The Sacrifice of Abraham*.)

Ou	[hu] for [u],
Malgré	[maləgre] for [malgre],
Parfaitement	[parəfɛtəmɑ̃] for [parfɛtmɑ̃],
Quel prix	[kɛlə pri] for [kɛl pri],
Vendre	[vɑ̃dərə] for [vɑ̃drə].*

[13]One can exercise by whispering, an easy means which spares the voice. (c

Stuttering is often corrected by the effect of the rhythm. The mind, drawn along by the feeling of the meter to say regularly a thing which it knows in advance, makes the organs obey without the least hesitation.

If the lips are flattened against the teeth, the voice will be better and the words more clear.

*[14]M. Michelot, our colleague, is the first to advise this exercise.

This method could lead to the doubling of all the consonants; but the correction of that fault is always easy.*

Mon fils, tu ne l'es plus
[mɔ̃f ist yn əl ɛpl y]
Va, ma haine est trop forte.
[vam a ɛn ɛtr ofɔrt ə]
D'Étéocle et de toi tous les droits sont perdus.
[det eɔkl ed ət wat ul edr was ɔ̃p ɛrd y]
Dans mon âme ulcérée, oui, la nature est morte.
[dɑ̃m ɔn ɑm yls er e ə wil an at yr ɛm ɔrt ə]
Ton frère et toi, je ne vous connais plus.
[tɔ̃fr ɛr et wa, ʒən əv uk ɔn ɛpl y]
Antigone me reste, Antigone est ma fille,
[ɑ̃t ig ɔn əm ər ɛst ə,ɑ̃t ig ɔn ɛm af ij]
Elle est tout pour mon coeur, seule elle est ma famille.
[ɛl ɛt up urm ɔ̃k œrs œl ɛl ɛm af am ij]
(Recitative in *Oedipe*.) [J]

In the exercise which we have just advised on the syllables, it is necessary to see only a special means of perfecting the mechanical faculties of the organs of articulation, and not the procedure to follow in the pronunciation of words joined with melody. (d

3. THE ACCENTS

The human voice offers the following four characteristics:

1. The variable duration of the sounds;
2. Their timbre;
3. Their raising or their lowering in the scale;
4. Their various degrees of intensity.

These characteristics, if one adds to them the variety of the consonants, the breaths [or quarter-rests], the strength and movement of the delivery, form the ensemble of elements which constitute the *accents* in the various languages.

In each idiom, one can easily discern various kinds of accents.

[K]

The *grammatical accent*, which distinguishes by their duration the long and short vowels (that is to say, which marks the quantity of them), and indicates in addition their open or closed timbre [translator's italics];

The *written accent*, or the graphic signs of the grammatical accent [translator's italics];

The *reasoned accent*, which makes evident the sense of the discourse and the relative importance of the ideas which make up the sentence. The punctuation, in our languages, serves in part to indicate this accent;

The *pathetic accent*, which is announced by the expression which the voice takes under the dominion of the strong passions. This accent unites with itself all the other characters which we have just enumerated.

Finally, the *national accent*.

We will restrict ourselves to the analysis of the grammatical and the pathetic accents, the only ones whose study may be in the scope of our subject.

4. QUANTITY, OR TONIC ACCENT

In individual speech, he who speaks, drawn by the rapid work of conception, stops only at one point of each word, at a single syllable which dominates all the others and on which is deployed the action of the organs. The burst which determines the importance of the privileged syllable constitutes what one calls *prosody* [translator's italics]. It is marked, in nearly all languages, on one single syllable of the word, however extended it might be, and it is produced only by a prolongation of duration.[15]

---

*[15]One can affirm *a priori* that all languages have one quantity. The need to express our sentiments in all their energy forces us to support [*d'appuyer*] the voice and to prolong it in the words which we want to render incisive. We stop on the most important vowel of the word.

To this prolongation is often added an elevation and a swelling of the voice, plus a particular sonority of the vowel; but there are four different elements which, although habitually found together, are not less perfectly distinct. The first constitutes only the prosodic accent, or the quantity.

To this aggregation of three elements on the same syllable is added a fourth: the sonority of the vowel; these four elements so distinct: the prolongation, the timbre, the intensity and the elevation, are generally confused under the name of *grammatic accents*. The two first functions are the only ones which constitute the grammatic accent, and it is necessary to submit to the actions of the signs names *acute accent*, *grave accent*, *circumflex accent*. As for the intensity and the elevation, it seems to us that one should consider them only as oratorical accents.

The characteristics of the grammatic accents thus distinguished, it will be easy to show that the graphic signs which represent these characteristics have not been submitted to any regular system.

First, the characteristics of the grammatic accent number only two: the duration and the timbre of the vowel; while the signs which represent them are three:

1. The acute accent. It serves only to determine the closed timbre and is applied exclusively to the vowel E. Example: *Bonté* [bɔ̃te];

2. The grave accent. It determines both the timbre and the duration of the vowels A and E. Examples: *Là* [la], *prophète* [prɔfɛt]. It has a uniform meaning relative to timbre in opening both vowels, but its action on the duration is double, since it shortens the A, and lengthens the E;

3. The circumflex accent. It determines equally both the timbre and the duration. Its action is contrary to that of the grave accent; it always lengthens the vowel, as in the words *âme* [ɑmə], *tête* [tɛtə], *gîte* [ʒitə], *dôme* [domə], *flûte* [flytə]; but sometimes it opens the timbre (*tête*, *gîte*), and sometimes it covers it (*âme*, *dôme*, *flûte*).*

A little attention will suffice to distinguish the accented syllable among all the other syllables of the word. Examples:

"...Nessun maggiore dolore
[nɛssun madʒɔre dolɔre]

"Che ricordarsi del Tempo felice
[ke rikɔrdarsi dɛl tɛmpo felitʃe]

"Nella miseria............" Dante.
[nella mizerja]

"Champs paternel, Hébron, douce vallée,
[ʃɑ̃ patɛrnɛl, ebrɔ̃, dusə valeə,]

"Loin de vous a langui ma jeunesse exilée," etc.
[lwɛ̃ də vu za lɑ̃gi ma ʒœnɛ sɛgzileə,]

All words have one accented syllable; the monosyllables themselves do not make exception to that rule; but the accentuation allows various nuances in proportion to the value of the words which compose the sentence. Also, the principal word receives, by reason of its importance, a more marked accent than those which surround it.[16]

5. THE STRESS OF THE CONSONANTS

In addition to the prosodic accent, one should take into consideration, in words, the stress of the consonants; that stress consists of a stronger and more slowly prepared impulse which carries principally on some particular consonants. Examples:

t m s p t p
Toujours, Méchant, Sempre, Troppo, etc.

---

*[16]See page 19 for the place that the prosodic accent can occupy in verse. See also *Les Vrais Principes de la Versification*, by Antonio Scoppa, Sicilien.*

This stress of the consonants corresponds to the quantity of the vowels.[17] *A single word can have one or several points of stress, or yet not present any; on the contrary, there is never in a single word but one syllable, and one single vowel of that syllable, which carries the tonic accent. Examples:

At...ten...to, af...fan...no, trop...po, af...flit...ta.

An...cora, sciagure.

Lare, soave.*

The first four words present two points of stress; the following two present only one; the last two have none.

The stronger stress of the consonant necessarily leads to increasing it; already Bacilly,[18] and later Bérard,[19] and Blanchet,[20] had felt this need of reinforcement. The first two speak of it expressly.

The two stresses of articulation could be denoted as *strong* and *weak*, and, like the accents, submitted, so to say, to a heirarchical ranking. These authors felt it so well that they were led to modify the orthography of the words and to write them thus:

```
    t               f
Des tourments d'un funeste amour...
```

---

[17]The stress of the consonant has caused some authors to believe that in addition to the principal accent of the long syllable, there was in some words a secondary accent.

*[18]*L'Art de bien chanter*, by B. D. Bacilly, Paris, 1668, p. 307.*

*[19]*L'Art du chant*, Paris, 1755, pp. 93, 99.*

*[20]*L'Art du chant*, Paris, 1756, pp. 55, 61.*

Since, this notation has been attempted, either by numbers or otherwise.[21] But the difficulty of interpreting the agreed upon signs has caused the abandonment of this appreciation to the intelligence of the singer.*

In what circumstances is it necessary to *stress* the consonants?

1. In order to surmount the mechanical difficulty of articulation;

2. In order to strengthen the expression of the sentiment;

3. In order to give more reach [*portée*] to the articulation in a huge room;

1. It is necessary to stress the syllabication when one wants to overcome the resistance which groups of consonants pose to the organs, whether by their number, or by their nature. This effort gives to the articulation the appropriate degree of energy and clarity.

This principle is applied more or less rigorously in the different languages. In Italian, every time one must articulate more than one consonant, whether the same consonant is repeated, or it is joined with different consonants, one separates the consonants with a stress which serves to prepare the second.

Examples: *Bella, troppo, *andremo,* sempre, risplendere,* which must be pronounced: Bel...la, trop...po, con...ten...to, *an...dremo,* sem...pre, ris...plendere, etc.

In French, one applies the same principle to the initial

---

[21]The renewal of these movements has been more recently attempted with the same objective by Vaccai.

consonant of a word when that consonant is found to be also the final consonant of the preceding word. Examples:

"Le soc-qui fend la terre."[22]

"L'hymen-n'est pas toujours entouré des flambeaux." (Racine.)

Il avait de plant vif-ferme cette ouverture." (La Fontaine.)

2. It is necessary to stress the articulation in order to appropriately strengthen the sentiment. All the energetically accented words have some effect on the soul, because they seem dictated by a *vital impression*. It is especially the important word of the phrase which should receive this stress. Examples: L

*[22]Marmontel, *Éléments de littérature*, III, 17. No author gives the rules for the point of stress.*

Mozart:
Don Giovanni,
Aria.

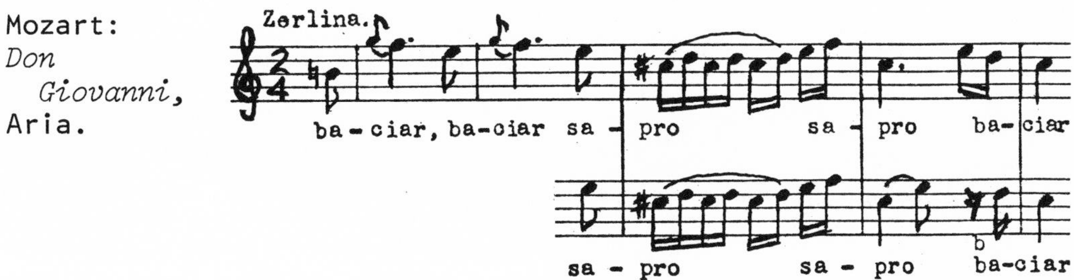

The well known phrase from the finale of the second act of Rossini's *Otello*:

owes half of its effect to the letters P, B and D. *If one would substitute a vowel for the initial sound of the second word in the line:

Rossini:
Guillaume Tell,
Trio.

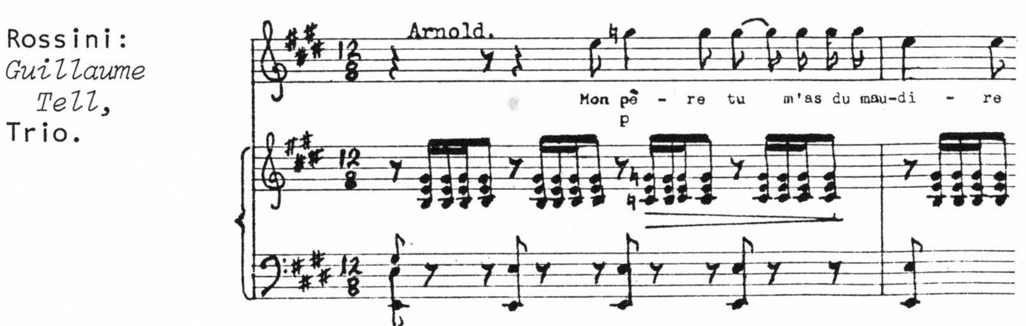

so that it is transformed thus: 

that heart-rending exclamation would immediately lose all its vigor; and never believe that it would suffice to yell more loudly in order to reinstate to the sound the value that it would receive from the consonant; no, the greatest burst of the voice deprived of that stress would lack the explosion which renders it incisive, and would vainly fatigue the singer.[23]*

Only the attack of the vowel by the *coup de glotte* can be so effective, but in more than one place, *as in the example which concerns us,* that manner would be out of place.

It goes without saying that this force of articulation on which we insist at such length should be in proportion to the character of the sentiment; according to the circumstances, the same word will have in its articulation different degrees of energy, and a word which would express a strong thought, if it includes only simple or weak consonants, will often call for a more vigorous articulation than some other which would contain double or hard consonants, but which expresses only a secondary detail.

3. Articulation being the most necessary element to an intelligible pronunciation, the need to be understood in general causes one to stress the consonants in proportion to the intensity of the voice, and the importance of the location; as a consequence, one stresses more strongly when one declaims than when one speaks, and still more strongly when one sings.

Without this increase of elasticity in the organs, the attack of the consonant, the penetration of the syllabication, disappear by the same fact as the intensity of the sound by the dispersion of the voice

---

[23]It is necessary to prevent with the greatest care the shocks which that impulsive force could give to the voice. Those shocks, if they should multiply, would have the effect of giving the voice a lachrymose character.

in a large area.[24]

Musically, the two elements of the word are associated with the two elements of the melody, the vowels with the tones, and the consonants with the meter. The consonant presents to the singer the same resources as the bow stroke or the tonguing offer to the instrumentalist. In fact, the consonant serves to mark the time, to make it incisive, to speed up or slow down the movement, to accentuate the rhythms. It specifies moreover, the instant when the orchestra must make its entrance and the bass part rejoin the voice, after an *ad libitum*, a conduit, an organ point; it is by the consonant, finally, that one takes up the tempo and the final cadence. One should always prepare the consonants in advance, in order that they may not strike too hard, in such a manner that the explosion always falls on the stroke of the time.

6. THE BREADTH OR HOLDING OF THE VOICE ON THE WORDS

When one sings music with words, if one does not know how to render the emission of the voice independent of the movements of the consonants, the organ receives a certain shock which destroys the intensity, the confidence, and the linking of the notes. In order to prevent these inconveniences, it is necessary, in the group of movements necessary to singing, to distinguish the nature of the functions and the mode of action of the four principal mechanisms of the vocal apparatus: *the *lungs*, the *glottis*, the *pharynx*, and the *organs of articulation*.*

---

[24]The sombre timbre, by obscuring the vowels, also contributes to the confusion of the pronunciation.

*The *lungs* have the function of stimulating and maintaining, by a measured and continuous current of air, the vibrations of the *glottis*.[25] This should be rigid and invariably the same in its dimensions as long as the same sound is prolonged, and change rapidly and precisely to a new state upon a change in intonation. The *pharynx*, in its turn, by sure and well calculated movements, will tune, to the benefit of the timbre which the dominant emotion requires, the two registers, the different parts of the range of the instrument and the various vowels. Finally, the *organs of articulation*, copying the precision of strong springs, will divide the sounds by marking the various consonants which will be met in the words.* When the singer knows *thus* how to make each apparatus function in the sphere *of action* which is peculiar to it, without disturbing the operation of the other apparatuses, the voice maintains all the parts of the performance, and connects all the different details of the melody in a full and continuous ensemble which constitutes the breadth of singing. If, on the contrary, one of the mechanisms does not properly fulfil its functions; if the chest is abrupt with, or stops breathing; if the glottis lacks rigidity and precision; if the pharynx shows discomfort or *inexperience*; if the organs of articulation, lacking suppleness, act in a soft [M] or incorrect manner, the voice comes out false, jerkily and with faulty quality; the pronunciation is defective and sometimes unintelligible. One says then that the singer lacks technique [*méthode*].

---

[25]We are saying here what the singer should do, though in reality the vocal cords are never maintained in a state of steady rigidity.

In addition to the dangers which a capable singer avoids, we can point out another no less serious. We want to talk about the *scrocco di voce*, in French, *couac* [squawk], a ridiculous burst of sound which, ordinarily, is heard in the chest tones placed above E for the tenors, and an octave higher in the head voice of the sopranos. If at the moment of articulating certain consonants or of vocalizing certain passages on these high notes, one neglects to support the expiration and the movements of the pharynx, the pharynx and the glottis, naturally forced to contract in order to produce these high notes, close completely, and the voice stops suddenly in order to reappear an instant later with an exaggerated or ridiculous explosion. [N]

From these general precepts, let us pass to some observations of detail. One should prolong the voice without shocks and without weakening from syllable to syllable, from one note to the note which follows, as if the aggregate formed only one equal and continuous sound. It is necessary to allot to the vowel the largest part of the value of the note which belongs to it, and to use only the end of that value in the preparation of the consonant which follows. [O]

That continuity of sound should not experience, because of the standing [*permanentes*] consonants, any interruption, however slight it may be. [P] The mute consonants are the only ones which completely stop the voice. Thus the [m] and [n][26] allow a nasal resonance to be heard:

---

[26]The passage through the mouth cavity being completely intercepted by the tongue in the case of the [n], and by the lips in the case of the [m].

co...nte...nto, m...ourir. The [l] produces two streams on the two sides of the tongue: *coll...e, l...anguir*,[27] [Q] etc.; and so on for the other consonants. [R] Until the time when the preparation begins, no consonant noise should be mixed in the voice, which will keep all its purity. The consonant should be pronounced only at the end of the syllable and of the tone.[28] Example: [S]

In rapid groups of notes, if that consonant is permanent (as opposed to mute), it communicates its quality on the entire last tone; *if it is mute, it takes from it half of its value.* Examples: [T].

---

[27]Without this help, the too-frequent interruptions would cut up the song and would make it appear thin and disjointed.

[28]Avoid saying : [laməpo, lunəgo, mesəta, istanəte, momenəto], etc.

Rossini: *Il Barbiere di Siviglia*, Cavatina.

Almaviva
oh is - - tan - te d'a - - mo - re fe - li - - ce mo - - men - - - to
oh is - ta - n-te me - - n-to

The same effect is not heard in the preparation of the [p], [k], [d] or [t].

We urge the student to practice on the pieces indicated below. They will solve the greatest difficulties in syllabication. (e

Arias for bass:
"Amor, amor, perchè mi pizzichi?" (Notes and words.) Fioravanti.
"A un dottor della mia sorte." (Notes and words.) (*Barber of Seville*.) Rossini.
"Largo al factotum della città." (Notes and words.) (*Barber of Seville*.) Rossini.
"Già l'insolito ardore." (Triplets.) (*Italian Girl in Algiers*.) Rossini.
"Si vada si sprezza la vita." (Fragment, triplets.) (*Thieving Magpie*.) Rossini.
"Vous me connaissez tous." (Notes and words.) (*Philtre*.) Auber.

Variations for Soprano:
"La biondina in gondoletta." (Third variation, triplets.) Paer.

Duet for Soprano and Tenor:
"Io ti lascio, io ti lascio." (Notes and words.) (*Secret Marriage*.) Cimarosa.

Duets for Soprano and Bass:
"Per piacere alla signora." (Notes and words.) (*Turk in Italy*.) Rossini.
"Come frenar il pianto." (Fragment, various difficulties.) (*Thieving Magpie*.) Rossini.
"Ah! di vender già parmi." (Fragment, triplets.) (*Corradino*.) Rossini.
"Quanto amore." (Notes and words.) (*Elixer of Love*.) Donizetti.
"Se dovessi prender moglie." (Various difficulties.) (*Italian Girl in Algiers*.) Rossini.

Duets for two Basses:
"Un segretto d'importanza." (Notes and words.) (*Cinderella*.) Rossini.
"D'un bel uso di Turchia." (Notes and words.) (*Turk in Italy*.) Rossini.

"Che l'antipatica vostra figura." (Notes and words.)
(*Clara of Rosemberg.*) Ricci.
"Mentra Francesco faceva il brodo." (Notes and words.) Coccia.

7. DISTRIBUTION OF THE WORDS UNDER THE NOTES

The simplest practical rule is that which shows how to apply one syllable to each isolated note, or to each group of slurred or beamed notes. This rule rests on this fact, that each syllable cannot be rendered by less than one note, whereas it can embrace an undetermined number of consecutive notes.[29] When each syllable is sung to a group of notes, these notes are joined by one or several beams if their value will permit that method, or by a slur if that value excludes the use of beams; in this latter case, each group represents only one syllable.

But, as the connections between the syllables and the notes are not always exactly indicated in the written music, in order to correct the errors which are encountered, one will have recourse to the fundamental principle that we formulate thus: have the common accent of the line fall on the down-beat of the second, third or fourth bar, according to the length of the phrase or member of the phrase relative to the verse.[30]

In fact, the composer himself, in the greatest number of cases,

---

[29]This rule permits one exception more apparent than real in a case of which we will speak presently. It is that in which the vowels are joined to form only one group.

[30]In order to understand this paragraph, it is indispensable to have the formation of the phrase in mind. (See Chapter II, section 1.)

has the common accent of the line fall on the down-beat of the second, third or fourth bar; and the reason for this is that these down-beats mark the limit of the member of the phrase or of the melodic line. Only the meeting of this down-beat with the common accent can indicate the rhythmic cadence. [U] *Also one never sees a weak syllable corresponding with this down-beat. The adjustment with which it is concerned will thus consist of replacing that accent on the beat which corresponds to it, then to place the other *necessary accents* of the line on the other strong beats, more rarely on weak beats.* Examples:

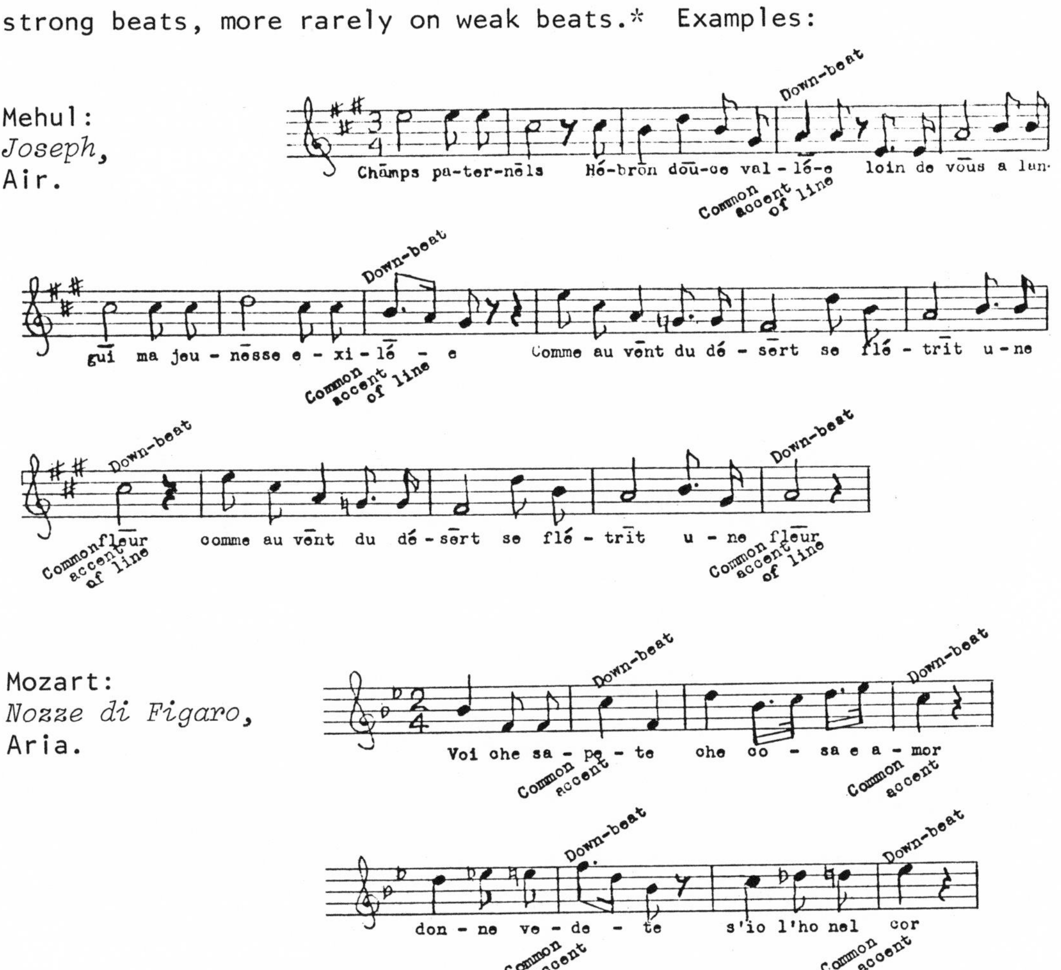

In the following aria of Handel, the translator has distributed the words badly. Handel: *Samson*, Aria.

The observation of this precept assumes the profound knowledge of the prosody of the language in which one sings, as well as of its laws of versification. V

*ITALIAN VERSE (f

Three principal laws preside over the formation of Italian Verse:

The first determines the quantity of syllables which come into each kind of verse;

The second fixes the number of long or accented syllables which must indispensably be found in each kind of line, and the places which they occupy [*numero e luogo degli accenti*]. It is primarily to this condition that Italian verse owes its rhythm which is so favorable to melody;

The third law distributes the rhymes. We will not have to concern ourselves with it.

The Italians count ten species of poetic lines; and as each line end on a smooth, transitory, or imperfect word, each specie of poetic line can also have three types (*piano*, *sdrucciolo*, or *tronco*). These species are distinguished by the name which expresses the number of syllables in the smooth line. Thus the transitory line and the imperfect line, although containing one syllable more or less than the smooth line, are counted like the smooth line. Examples:

Già di monti le cime s'indorano	(eleven syllables, transitory line.)
E di perle di tremulo gielo	(ten syllables, smooth line.)
Ogni rosa conchiglia si fà	(nine syllables, imperfect line.)

Before indicating the number and specific distribution of the accents, let us point out that in each line there is always one accent, namely, the final, which is subjected to an invariable rule. That accent consistently falls on the penultimate syllable of the *smooth* line, consequently on the third-to-the-last syllable of the *transitory* line, and on the final syllable of the *imperfect* line. Thus, for example, if the line is endecasyllabic (eleven syllables), the final accent will fall on the tenth syllable of the smooth line. This accent, because of its universality, has received the name of *common accent*. Let us pass to the rules which the other accents follow.

Endecasyllabic verse. In addition to the common accent on the tenth syllable, it takes another on the sixth. One may neglect this latter, but on the condition that two others be substituted for it, one on the fourth, and one on the eighth syllable. This variation of the rhythmic system is seen moreover in other species of lines. Apart from these indispensable accents, all occupy arbitrary places. We will content ourselves with giving a few examples of them, and for brevity, we will mark by numbers the various positions of the accents.

ENDECASYLLABIC
corresponding to French
lines of 10 syllables.
6 - 10
4 - 8 - 10
2 - 4 - 8 - 10

6 10
"Canto l'armi pietose e il capitano
4 8 10
"Che il gran sepolcro liberò di Cristo."
2 4 6 8 10
"Levommi il mio pensiero imparte ov' era
2 4 8 10
"Colei ch'io cerco e non ritrovo in terra."

DECASYLLABIC
corresponding to French
lines of 9 syllables.
6 - 9; 3 - 6 - 9

4 9
"Voi che sapete che cosa è amor."
3 6 9
"Non più andrai farfallone amoroso."

NOVENARIO
corresponding to French
lines of 8 syllables.
4 - 8
2 - 5 - 8

4 8
"A duro stral di ria ventura
4 8
"Misero me son posto a segno."
2 5 8
"Tormento crudele tiranno
2 5 8
"Mi strugge, e mi lacera il core."

OTTONARIO
corresponding to French
lines of 7 syllables.
3 - 7
3 - 5 - 7

3 7
"Sovrà il sen la man mi posa."
3 7
"Casta diva che innargenti."
3 7
"Che soave zeffiretto."
3 7
"Di piacer mi balza il cor."
3 5 7
"V'è la fresca e limpid' onda
3 5 7
"Che il tuo labbro invita a ber."

SETTENARIO
corresponding to French
lines of 6 syllables.
2 - 4 - 6

2 4 6
"Assisa al piè d'un salice."
2 4 6
"Fra poco a me ricovero."

SENARIO corresponding to French lines of 5 syllables. 2 - 5	2 5 "Tornate sereni 2 5 "Begli astri d'amore 2 5 "La speme balen 2 5 "Nel vostro dolore."
QUINARIO corresponding to French lines of 4 syllables. - 4	4 "Voi che sapete 4 "Che cosa è amor." 4 "Finche han dal vino 4 "Calda la testa."
QUADRISYLLABIC corresponding to French lines of 3 syllables. - 3	3 "Che soave 3 "Zeffiretto 3 "Questa sera 3 "Spirerà."
TRISYLLABIC corresponding to French lines of 2 syllables. - 2	2 "Se cerca 2 "Se dice 2 "L'amico 2 "Dov'è 2 "L'amico 2 "Infelice 2 "Rispondi 2 "Morì."

It is known that the common accent and that which results from the caesura are the only ones imperiously required in French verse. The regular use of other accents would make it as melodious as Italian verse.*

In stating that each syllable cannot be rendered by less than one note, we have not forgotten a particular case which seems to present a departure from that principle, but which one can easily reconcile to it. [W]

In order to recognize in which cases one should run the vowels together, and in which cases to the contrary, one must isolate them, it is necessary to consider the place which the tonic accent occupies. If any group of vowels is without an accent, the voice should not fix itself on any of them; if there is an accent in the group, it is the accented vowel which dominates; as a consequence the voice should glide equally over all the others, joining them into a single emission. That vowel can be found placed at the beginning, in the middle, or at the end of the group. Examples with two vowels: [X]

Examples with three vowels:

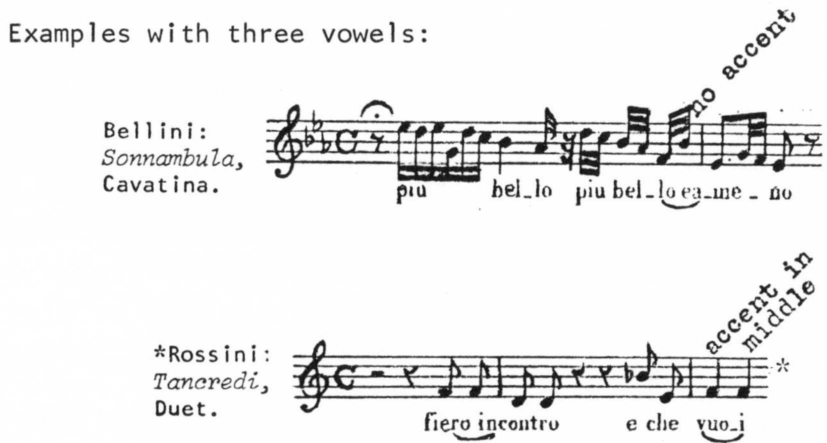

In the following groups of three vowels, there are no accents.

Examples with four consecutive vowels:

This contraction of several vowels into a single emission is one of the principal difficulties which hampers those to whom the singing of Italian is foreign.

*When the tonic accent falls on the first vowel of the group, one separates it from the others. In the words: *IsA...ura, gemE...a,* we separate the A from the u, and the E from the a, because the tonic accent is placed on the first vowel. Now, in a similar case the accented vowel keeps its value as a syllable, and is distinguished from the vowel or vowels which follow. It would be the same if the accent fell on one of the middle vowels. The word *giOia* furnishes us an example of that: the voice stops on the vowel O of that word, and slides *with an equal movement* over all the others.*

Sometimes one separates adjacent vowels of two words which follow each other in order to take a breath.

Mozart: *Clemenza di Tito*, Aria.
Breath
di - scen - da I - me - ne di - scen-da I - me - ne

Each vowel should be formed distinctly, but not at all detached by a jerk. Only the mouth instantaneously modifies the tone which the larynx emits without the latter articulating a different note for each vowel, and also the linking of the vowels being accompanied by an effect like that of a yawn.

It is necessary to assume that the note which carries the two or three vowels is divided into as many fractions which succeed each other without interval. *In order to demonstrate this rule more clearly, we write the passages seen above thus:*

*The contraction takes place within the same word, or from one word to the following word, and allows one to avoid hiatus. See the examples:

Che farò senza Euridice,

Bel raggio lusinghiere.*

*In these examples, *senza Euridice* and *raggio lusinghiere*, the vowels AEU [aeu], IO [dʒo], and IE [jɛ], have been contracted. In the first examples, as there is no accent, the voice glides over all the vowels.*

When the vowel is repeated, we have recourse to elision, which is only a kind of contraction. [Y]

As much as possible, the distribution of the syllables for the melody should be done in such a manner that they mark the measures with regularity. One will depart from this principle only when its application would present obvious inconveniences.

*Rossini: *Semiramide*, Cavatina.

The need to facilitate the emission of the voice and the clarity of the vocalization forces one to break this rule and to choose among the words some words or syllables more favorable to the effect, and that one repeat without keeping strictly to a regular order.

Here are the various cases which may occur:

1. When one encounters a rather lengthy [*développé*] passage, one must choose, in order to perform it, the open vowels [a], [ɛ], [ɔ]. These vowels give the organ attractiveness and facility.[31] Examples:

Mozart: *Don Giovanni*, Aria.

---

[31]This precept extends to all the idioms, to the French language as well as to all the others.

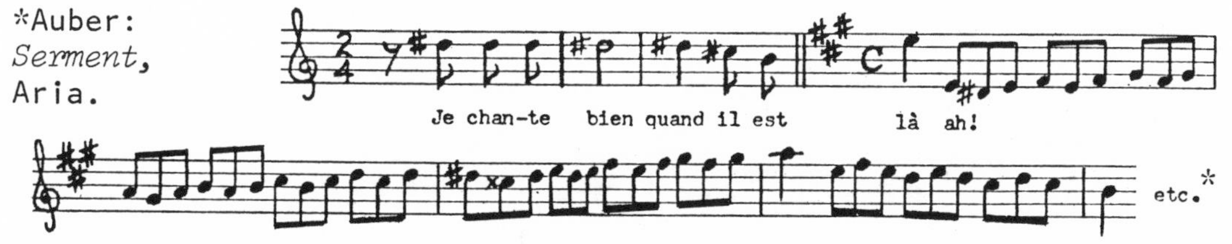
*Auber:
Serment,
Aria.
Je chan-te bien quand il est là ah!
etc.*

2. When multiple syllables too frequently cut a passage and tend to dull the voice, it is better to unite the entire passage into a single syllable. The variant of the passage below can serve as an example:

Rossini:
Barbiere,
Cavatina.
Rosina.
e cento trappo - le fa - - rò fa - rò gio - car
Variant:
e cento trap-po - le fa - rò fa - rò gio - car
fa-rò gio-car .... fa - rò gio - car
fa-rò gio-car .... gio - car

3. Sometimes one succeeds in freeing the performance only by omitting some words. [Z]

*Mercadante:
Andronico,
Duet.
Vo fe - li - ce a tri - on - far vo fe - - li - ce a tri - on - far
vo a tri - - - - on - far
vo............a................tri-on - far
*

*In the cavatina from the *Barber of Seville*, the disposition differs essentially from the written order. In the duet from *Andronico* the line is divided; this license seems permissible to us since it modifies the meaning only slightly. Moreover the line has already been heard in its entirety, and it is repeated only for the need of the music. The form that we propose offers a double advantage: it places the roulades on the vowels [o] and [a], and it avoids the need to articulate the syllable *tri* on the high *B*.*

The following dispositions also permit the avoidance of articulations on high notes.

*Rossini: *Siege de Corinthe*, Aria.

Rossini: *Cenerentola*, Rondo.

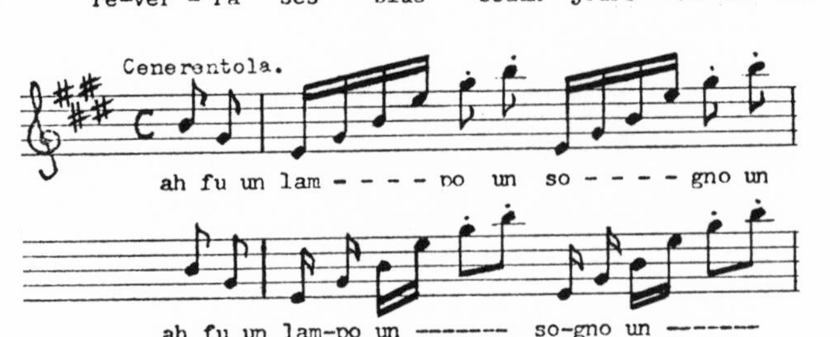

Rossini: *Donna del lago*, Rondo.

Except in cases of the same nature as these, one will avoid distributing the syllables in an unequal and irregular manner.

4. If the syllabication occurs on notes that are too high and one can do nothing to change the words, one will try to have the high tones preceded by an ascending portamento, but this portamento must be in accord with the musical sense. Examples:

*Donizetti: *Anna Bolena*, Aria. Donizetti: *Lucia*, Aria.

Support would be useless if one would attack the B *in falsetto register.*

The voice thus placed on the high note by means of the portamento, one can change syllables more easily than if it were necessary to attack the syllable and the note at the same time.

5. In order to avoid syllabication on a high note, one can also have recourse to a lower grace note conveniently placed, on which one articulates the sýllable in advance. [AA] Example:

Donizetti: *Lucia,* Rondo.

The placement of the syllable on the lower grace note permits the organ to attain, by means of a light and rapid portamento, the high note, and on the first instant of that value.

In some cases one can again facilitate the attack of the high note if one takes advantage of the light internal sound which the preparation of certain consonants produces, that of the [m], the [n], the [d], the [b], etc., for example.[32] This sound, preceding by an instant the explosion of the voice, permits one to attempt the tone accurately and with a firmness of the glottis, and removes the danger of producing what one calls a *couac* [squawk]. Examples:

*Rossini: *Mahomet,* Aria. *

Donizetti: *Anna Bolena,* Aria.

---

[32]See footnote number 4.

The alteration of the vowel in certain syllables is a convenient resource.[33] Example:

Weber:
Robin des bois,
Aria.
veil-le grand Dieu veille sur son re - tour
veil-le grand Dueu sur son

The I [j] has been changed into a U [ɥ].

Moreover, in whatever manner the voice takes it, the organ will always be able to approach these difficult notes with success, provided it is not caught off guard, but that at the moment of producing them, it is properly positioned; that is the only aim of the various procedures which we indicate.

8. OBSERVATIONS

In the rules which precede, we have presented the modifications introduced in the prescribed order, which have for their objective the facilitation of the performance. We are going to concern ourselves with other alterations introduced in the aim of adding to the vigor, and of completing the effectiveness of the singing.

We will speak of the repetition, or of the insertion of a word or a phrase.

1. Repetition has the aim of strengthening the expression.

---

[33]See pages 2-12.

Examples of repetition:

Mozart: *Don Giovanni*, Recitative.

*Rossini: *Gazza ladra*, Aria. *Coppola: *Nina*, Cavatina.

2. The teacher and the singer have the liberty of adding, if the meaning permits it, one of the monosyllables: *ah, yes, no,* whether it be for adding to the number of syllables, or to replace others.

*In the example following, in place of making the fermata on the syllable *mi,* as in number 1, one introduces the exclamation *Ah!* and articulates the phrase as in example 2.*

*Rossini: *Tancredi*, Cavatina.

N°2.
co - ro - na-te ah! il mio va - - lor

Bellini: *Sonnambula,* Cavatina.

na-tu-ra na-tu-ra non non bril-lo non bril-lo
tu-ra non bril - lo ah non brillo

*We still have, in certain cases, the option of restoring to the word which ends in one of the liquid consonants, [l], [m], or [r], that is to say, to the unfinished word, the syllable which has been removed from it. Thus, of *cor* [kɔr], one will make *core* [kɔre]; of *bel* [bɛl], *bello* [bɛllo]. (See *Traité de Versification*, by Scoppa.)[34] This syllable permits the placement of more stress, and characterizing with more emphasis the penultimate syllable. Sometimes, on the contrary, one supresses it. Examples:*

*Rossini: Tancredi, Cavatina.
Tancredi.
ah! il mio va - - lore
*Bellini: Norma, Cavatina.
Norma.
tem - pra an co - ra tempra au cor lo ze-lo au-da-ce

The rules which we have just posed for the Italian language apply equally to singing French, with the exception always of the last.

---

*[34]The monosyllables *il, del, al, dal, con, non,* and *per* are exempt from this rule.*

CHAPTER II

THE ART OF PHRASING [A]

The art of phrasing occupies the highest point in the science of singing. It embraces the search for all the effects, and the proper means of producing them. In order to excell in it, the singer must add to a *complete and irreproachable mechanism* the knowledge of the difficulties and of the material arrangements which the performance presents.

Tones do not express, like words, precise ideas, but simply evoke sensations; one understands that a given melody can be bent to very diverse expressions, according to the different ways of accenting it. The instrumentalist possesses a very wide liberty as to the expression and the ornaments; and if one excludes some accents determined in advance which the harmonic progressions, appoggiaturas, held tones, syncopations and songs of a very pronounced rhythm take, the performer is almost entirely free to express in the melody that color which pleases him, provided he confines himself to the general character of the piece. The effects of the vocal melody leave much less room for discretion; they are determined in part by the long syllables which always dominate singing, and finally by the expression of the words, which fixes the general character of the melody. However, these conditions do not suffice to decide in an invariable manner the meaning and the expression of a song; a great part still remains up to the inspiration and the ability of the artist.

The principal elements of the art of phrasing will be treated under the titles:

Pronunciation;

The formation of the phrase;

Respiration;

Time [*mesure*];

Dynamics [*forte-piano*];

Ornaments;

Expression.

Without the joining of these diverse elements, there is no complete musical performance.

What we have to say on the pronunciation has already been presented in the preceding chapter, under the title of *Articulation in Singing*. We will not come back to it.

Before entering into the examination of the other means which the art of phrasing embraces, we are going to explain briefly the formation of the musical phrase; the study of this very important point teaches us to distinguish the ideas which compose a melody, and thereby prepares us to use the respiration appropriately; it serves to make us discern the portions of the musical thought which simply call for the loud or soft from those which require besides, the use of ornaments, etc.

1. THE FORMATION OF THE PHRASE

Music, like language, has its prose and its verse. One knows that the writer of prose is not at all subjected to all the difficulties which annoy the poet. The rhyme, the caesura, the limited number of feet, the regular cadence of the accents, are the fetters, and also the special graces of poetry.

Neither does melodic prose insist on any count of the number of measures, on the symmetry of the cadences, often not even on the regularity of the time; for example:

The *Psalm XLII* of Marcello, for bass: "*Dal tribunal augosto.*"

The *Largo* in the *Convitto d'Alessandro*, of Handel: "*Ahi! di spirti turba immensa.*"

The Palestrina-like choruses, plainsong, recitative.

This last kind of melodic prose obeys only the accents of prosody and the change of the emotion.

In what I would call *melodic verse*, on the contrary, the most perfect regularity governs. Here the rhythmic instinct exercises an absolute empire. In order to satisfy it, one establishes a complete symmetry between the different parts of the melody, one confines them within certain time limits which are marked by easily understood resting places; in this manner, the ear can, without uncertainty, recognize each element of the phrase, the same as it recognizes the accents, the caesura, the rhyme, etc., in verse.

The first question which we have to ask ourselves now is this: What are the measurements of melodic verse? *In order to answer this question, we have only to recall the principles which govern with regard to verse properly so-called. Lines of twenty to twenty-five syllables would obviously be only prose; our ear could not find in lines of such length the rhythm of poetry. The same disadvantage would not be produced if, in place of extending the length of the line, one would abridge it to excess, for the lively and accentuated rhythm of lines of three and four syllables pleases the ear, especially as one can easily rejoin them to form of them lines of six or eight syllables.[35] Finally, if in poetry each line would present a different length, this too-varied succession would not have any rhythmic charm; it would be reduced to the effect of prose.

All that we have just said about poetry applies to music.*

If the melodic phrase were developed to too great a length, the feeling of the rhythm would be lost for the ear, and the form of the line would disappear.

If, on the contrary, the phrase were cut by frequent rests, our instinct, obeying certain laws which govern it without our knowledge, would experience the need to rejoin these fragments in order to compose regular phrases of them. Examples:

Rossini:
Cenerentola,
First Finale.
zitto zitto piano piano senza strepi_to e ru_more
Handel:
Rinaldo,
Aria.
Collection de chants classiques by L.B.C.
Larghetto.
lascia chio pianga la du_ra sor_te

*Finally, if one would accumulate a series of melodic lines of different lengths, the ear, deprived of its necessary guide, the symmetry, would once more lose all impression of the rhythm and of the meter. Let us notice however that the rhythmic accent, that precious

---

35See Scoppa, *Op. cit.*, Part I, p. 260, note 1.

resource of the composer, is not always indispensable to him, and that he can, by neglecting it, sometimes obtain beauties of the first order; this is what the *Psalm XLII* of Marcello, the largo pieces of Handel, *Tutta raccolta in me*, and *Ahi! di spirti*, etc., prove. The grandiose expression which characterizes these pieces could not be surpassed by any regular rhythm.*

These generalities established, let us pass on to the details.

In order to measure with precision a melody or the parts which compose it, we have recourse to a series of regularly spaced percussions marking what are called the *beats* of the measure. But this series of successive beats, if they were constantly the same, would produce, after some moments, only a vague and monotonous impression. In order to escape this uniformity, one gives to certain beats of the succession, symmetrically spaced, a stress, a more characterized accent. The beats accented in that fashion, which are called *strong beats*, in opposition to the unaccented beats, which are called *weak beats*, serve to group the beats by two or three, and to form the two elementary measures which are the basis of all the others (the *binary* measure, formed of a strong beat and a weak beat, and the *ternary* measure, formed of a strong beat and two weak ones). With the aid of these accents, the ear easily distinguishes the groups which are attached to them and counts as many measures as there are first beats perceived by it.[36] [B]

---

[36]Let us notice that the beats [*temps*] whose function is simply to determine the movement can be complete only when a second stroke [*percussion*] is heard, so that each beat is always enclosed between two strokes. Likewise, the measure, which has for its objective the group-

The length of a measure confined between two down-beats constitutes a *member of the phrase.*

The measure, in its turn, plays with regard to the melody the role of marking the simple time. Here again the ear, in order to grasp a large number of details in one stroke, joins these measures themselves by twos or by threes, and there is thus formed a new binary or ternary measure of a higher order. The slightest attention suffices to cause one to be struck by the analogy which exists between the joining of several beats constituting a measure, and the aggregation of several measures constituting a musical thought. In order to understand well a musical thought, we need to be struck at equal intervals by more vigorous accents, which, by grouping themselves, offer to our ear new points of reference. These accents, of a nature still more characteristic than those of the measure, are formed by the cooperation of the harmony and the resting places, and serve to group the measures by two or by three, one strong and one weak, or else one strong and two weak. It is this last extent of two or three measures enclosed between three or four first beats that is usually called the *musical phrase*, and that we have called the *melodic line* [*vers mélodique*]. Examples: [C]

Rossini:
Gazza ladra,
Cavatina.
Minetta.
tut_to sor _ ri_de_re mi veggo in tor _ _ no
phrase member
phrase member
phrase

---

ing of the beats by two or by three is complete only after the stroke of the initial beat of the following measure. Only then does the ear recognize the kind of measure which governs the piece.

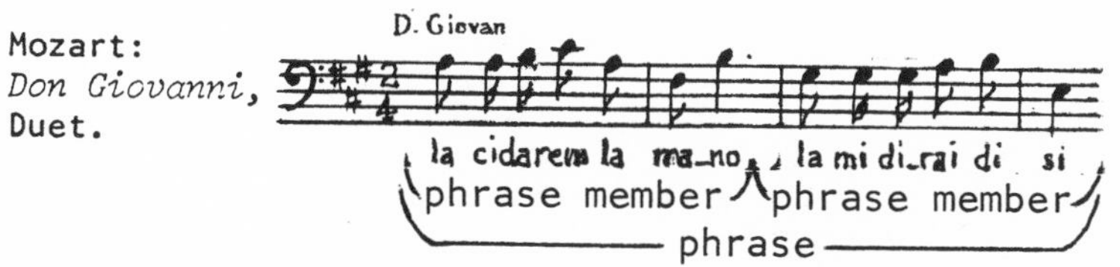

Having arrived at this point, it is a highest instinct which guides us; it is the feeling of the symmetry and of the rhythmic cadence applied to large divisions of the melody. *Example:*

*The dimensions of the phrase are naturally confined in limits laid out on a higher level, limits which one cannot go beyond, and which one also could not excuse oneself from attaining. If they are extended beyond, or if they fall short of the mark, the ear, by instinctive need for compensation, divides into two the phrases which are too long,[37] and joins into a single line those which lack length. It is to satisfy this requirement of the ear that in slow movements one ordinarily establishes a resting place at the second measure. Example:

C *In lively movements, the feeling can permit up to eight or nine measures.* Examples:

---

[37]It is the same principle which we apply to the measure of time. We divide each beat of largo and adagio movements by two or four, while we unite into two strong beats the movements of church music, and into one the *allegro vivace* movements in triple time. Examples: the *Largo* from Haydn's *Stabat Mater*; the Introduction from Semiramide, "Freme il tempo"; the Quintet from the *Barber*, "Birbanti, bricconi."

By reflecting a moment, one recognizes that these phrases have, in reality, only the length of three or four measures performed in an ordinary tempo. Examples:

The resting places of the phrases have been given the name of *half-cadence*. *(See Reicha.)*

A single phrase would give only a vague and isolated impression. That impression, in order to be precise and complete, should recur by the return of a phrase of the same length as the first. The comparison which the ear instinctively makes between the two successive phrases brings about the idea of symmetry, and as a consequence, of rhythmic cadence. The joining of these two phrases is the least development that the musical *period* can receive.

An example of the melodic period follows:

Mozart:
Don Giovanni,
Duet.
D. Giovanni
La ci darem la ma-no la nidi-rai di si
ve di non è lon - ta-no par-tiam mio ben da qui
Zerlina
Vor-
rei e non vor- re-i mi tre-ma un po-co il cor fe- li-ce ver sa-
re-i ma puo bur-lar mi an-cor ma puo bur-lar mi an-cor

In regularly cadenced music, one does not join phrases of different lengths; only prose includes them.

Various Observations.

Before and after the first beats of the measures, one must have noticed several notes; they are indispensable in order to fulfil the melody: they permit the distribution of the syllables which are weak or charged with less important accents; they are a component part of the melodic design, but they do not fulfil the rhythmic cadence; they are, so to speak, only an appendage of the initial beats. We will call them *complementary notes*. Here are some new examples of them:

*Mozart:
Don Giovanni,
Aria.
Da Elvira.
ah! chi mi di - ce ma-i quel barba-ro do - v'è
Rossini:
Gazza ladra,
Cavatina.
Ninetta.
tut-to sor - ri-de-re mi veggo in - tor - - no

One must also have noticed in some examples rests placed as early as in the first measure, often even after the second note, as in these:

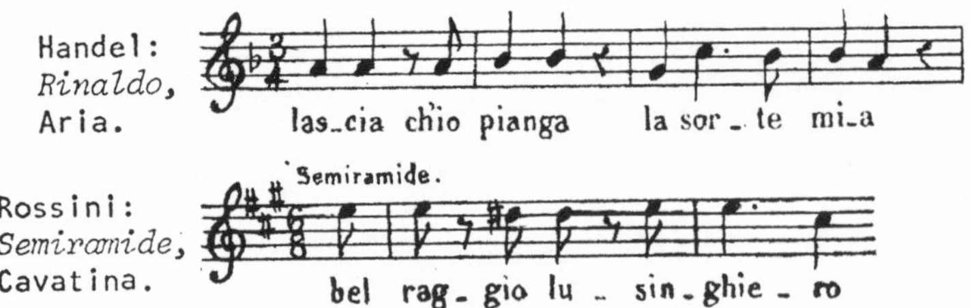
Handel:
Rinaldo,
Aria.
las-cia ch'io pianga la sor - te mi-a
Semiramide.
Rossini:
Semiramide,
Cavatina.
bel rag - gio lu - sin - ghie - ro

In all these cases, the sigh makes an integral part of the motive; it indicates an expressive accent, and not a rest. These two or three notes form melodic *motives*.

The motive is in each phrase the shortest distribution of values which can represent an idea. In order to form a motive, there must be at least two notes.[38] The motives are separated from each other by some difference which distinguishes the end of one motive from the beginning of another. This difference consists of a little rest (examples A), of the use of one note of longer value (example B), or of the return of the same melodic group, that is to say, of the same values or of the same intervals (examples C).[39]

Semiramide.
A
Motive
Motive
A
Motive
*Rossini:
Semiramide,
Cavatina.
bel rag-gio lu singhie-ro
lascia ch'io pianga
tut - to
sor
*
Nina.
B
Motive
Coppola:
Nina,
Rondo.
co me mai nel nuo - vo in - can - to

---

*[38]See Reicha, *Traité de mélodie*.*

[39]In general, dotted notes, triplets, groups of four, six, eight, sixteen, etc., notes, are motives.

In the sketch which we have just given of the musical phrase, the words which have precise meanings are:

Time,

Measure,

Member of the phrase,

Melodic line or phrase.

Those of which the meaning, because of their nature, remains a little vague and indefinite, are:

Rhythm,

Motive.

The word *rhythm* represents, not the material part, the form of the idea, but that impression produced by the periodic accents of the movement and of the intervals. The *motive*, according to whether its form is accented and lively, or slow and without character, serves to strengthen or to weaken the rhythmic movement. One also says of a motive that it is very rhythmic when the dominant value in it is short and incisive *(examples A).* One says on the contrary that it lacks rhythm when those same values are slow and without accent *(example B).*

Almost always, different motives are met at the same time in one piece. The orchestra, for example, sounds one or several, while the voices present entirely different ones.

Good melodies are, like speeches, divided by points of rest. The rests, as we have just explained, are regulated by the distribution and length of the partial ideas which comprise the melody. However, in certain circumstances, the period is developed without presenting a single rest, without the uniform movement of the notes being interrupted anywhere. [D] Examples:

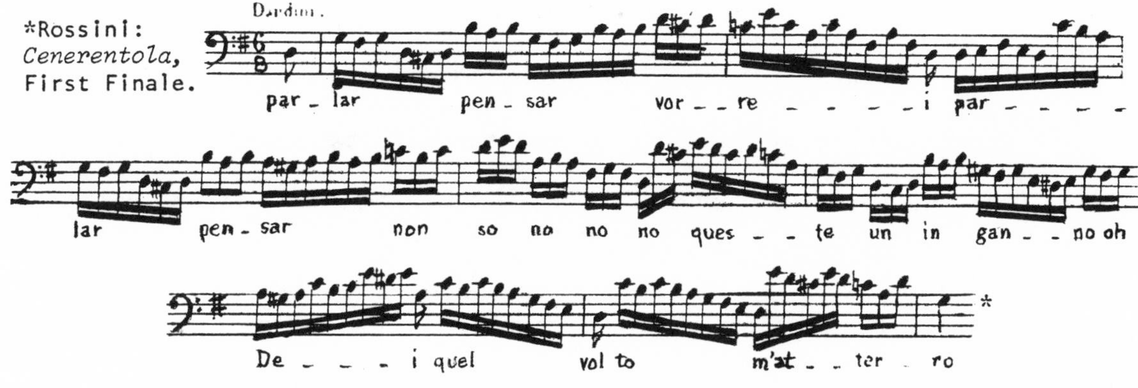

*Rossini: *Cenerentola,* First Finale.

However the ear easily recognizes the places where one could introduce rests; for example:

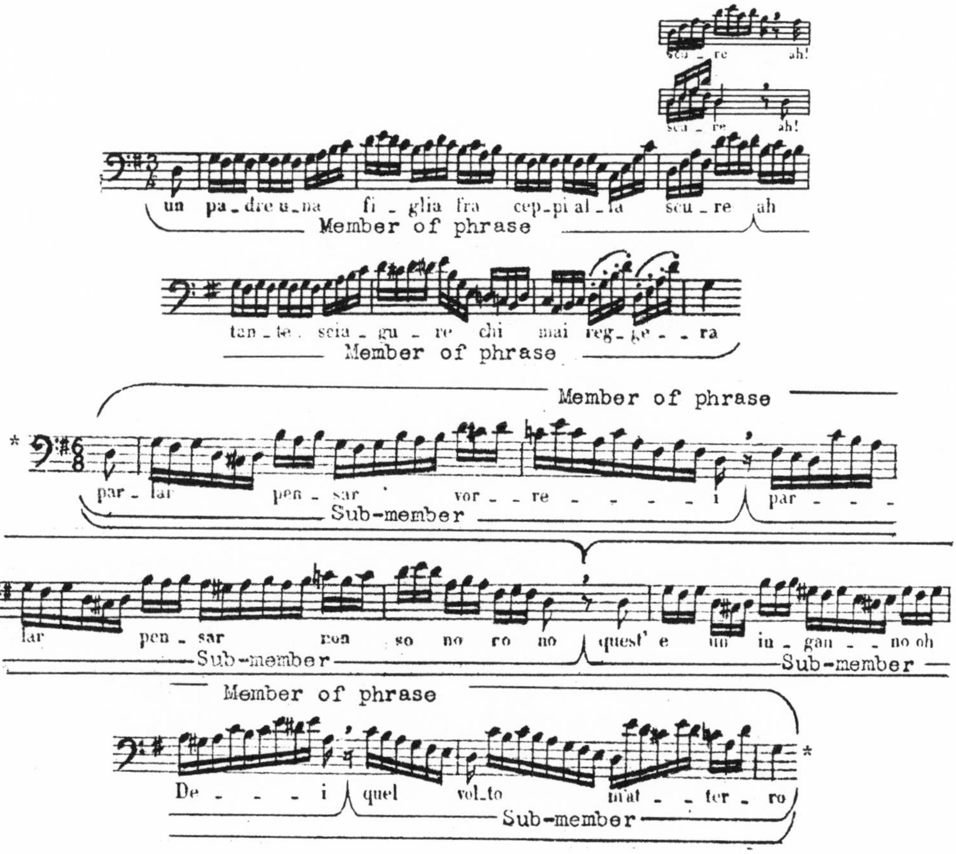

sca - re ah!

sca - re ah!

un pa - dre u - na fi - glia fra cep - pi al - la scu - re ah

Member of phrase

tan - te scia - gu - re chi mai reg - ge - - ra

Member of phrase

Member of phrase

* par - lar pen - sar vor - - re - - - - - i par - - -

Sub-member

lar pen - sar non so no ro no quest' e un in - gan - - no oh

Sub-member Sub-member

Member of phrase

De - - - i quel vol - to m'at - - ter - ro *

Sub-member

The little rest in the fourth measure, which interrupts the equal movement of the sixteenth notes, suffices to mark in the two periods the two different members of the phrase. *One could, by means of similar rests, find the four sub-members of the first example.* It is always easy to cut in this manner the uniform movement of notes, as also to re-establish it in the case where it has been cut.

All the rests which we have just indicated belong exclusively to the melody combined with the harmony, and are completely distinct from those which the words permit, although they should agree with these latter.

We do not propose to follow the phrase in all the varieties that it can offer; this research should be the special objective of the composer. It suffices for us to have indicated the principle on which that part of the science rests. The instinct of the student, or an attentive study of the rhythm and of the cooperation of the harmony and the melody will supply what our exposition may have omitted.

Let us actually pass to the different parts of the art of phrasing.

2. BREATHING

It is indispensable, for the singer, to properly take and control his breath; for breathing is, so to speak, the regulator of singing. It is during the rests that one should breathe, but only during the rests which occur in the words and in the melody at the same time. These rests must be introduced even when the composer may not have written them; they serve, either to better emphasize the distribution of ideas, or to make the performance easier. The breaths should fall only on the weak beats, or on the weak parts of the strong beats, or better still at the end of the note which ends the motive; which permits attacking the following note at the beginning of its value, and keeping the accent of the measure intact.

As the rests which separate the phrases and the members of the phrases are longer than those which separate the motives, it is also these longer rests which one should choose to take a large breath. The shortness of the rests which separates the motives permits the taking only of very short breaths, and which one names, for that reason, *half-breaths* [*mezzi respiri*]. They are rarely written; it is up to the singer to place them appropriately. The following examples satisfy the various rules which we have just placed:

*Mozart: *Don Giovanni*, Aria.

*Rossini: *Gazza ladra*, Aria.

Mozart:
Don Giovanni,
Aria.
Zerlina.
batti battio bel ma_zet_to la tua po_ve_ra Zer_li_na sta_ro
ma_zet_to la tua Zer_li_na sta_ro
qui come a gnel_li_na le tue botte ad as_pet_tar
li_na le tue
*Rossini:
Semiramide,
Introduction.
Assur.
al suo tro no il succes so_ _re la re_
gi_ _na scie_gliera si la re_gi_ _na scie_glie ra
scie_gliera la re_
Mozart:
Don Giovanni,
Aria.
finch'han dal vi_no cal_da la tes_ta u_na grau fes_ta fa pre_pa_rar se tro_vi_in
tes_ta
piazza qualche ra_gazza te_co ancor quel_la cer_ca me_nar te_co ancor quella cer_ca me_nar
gazza
me_nar
me_nar
cer_ca me_nar cer_ca me_nar senza alcun or_dine la dauza si_a
me_nar me_nar

By introducing rests as we have just prescribed, one keeps the means of renewing his strength and of finishing the phrases with their full effect.

It will be permitted in certain cases, in order to increase the effect of a phrase, to join the diverse members of it by omitting the pauses which separate them. Examples:

*Rossini: *Italiana in Algieri*, Rondo.

ri-ve-der le pa triea-re - - - ne nel pe-riglio
&c.*
a-re - - - ne nel pe-riglio
&c.
&c.

Donizetti: *Anna Bolena*, Cavatina.

del mio pri-mi-e-ro a-mo - re ah non a ves sa il pet to
a-mo - re ah

We have just seen that one sometimes joins the members by omitting the silences that separate them to extend the melodic effect; other times, on the contrary, in order to make the melody more lively and free, one marks all the rests of the motives, whether by breathing each time, or by simply stopping the tone without breathing; which is in some circumstances, an express obligation. Examples:

Allegro.
Pacini:
Niobe,
Cavatina.
i tuoi fre_quen_ti pal_pi_ti

Allegretto
Meyerbeer:
Crociato,
Cavatina.
etc.
ah figlian_zioso il cor il cor t'al_tende anzioso t'attende t'attende il

cor deh vola ra_pi_do non tardar.

In the above examples, the rest or the mark (°) indicates the obligation to leave the note as soon as one has taken it, and not the right to breathe.

When two members of a phrase, or even two notes are joined by a portamento, and it is necessary to breathe between the two phrases or the two notes, one will breathe only after having executed the portamento; then one will attack the second note. Examples:

Rossini: *Gazza ladra*, Cavatina.

All° Ninetta.
quan_ti con ten_ti sí al_fin go_dro tut_to sor_ri_de_re

Rossini: *Sigismondo*, Cavatina.

qual niag_gior fe_li_ci_tà piu nen sen_te le sue pe_ne

Outside of the cases which we have just indicated, one cannot breathe without committing a fault.

The singer must measure his breath so as not to be forced to take more in the middle of a word or else between two words narrowly joined by the meaning. Often, in sustained songs, there are presented only a few rather long rests in order to permit taking a complete breath: if one lets them escape, one will be impeded [*gené*] through the entire piece. *Examples:*

*Rossini:
Guillaume Tell
Romance.

*Bellini:
Norma
Cavatina.

Sometimes, however, in phrases badly constructed for rests, one can be obliged to cut a word, a thought by a breath; but then the singer must conceal this liberty with enough skill that it completely escapes the notice of the listener. Its betrayal by a noise, by a ritard, by a movement of the body, would be to commit a grave fault. Example:

*Bellini: *Beatrice*, Duet.

After one has converted the point (A) into a breath of a value of one beat, there are presented nothing more than half breaths.

*The lack of time to breathe and the vigor which the passage requires can also oblige the singer to breathe during the time of the syllable *ra*; it is before the *g* (B) that one should be permitted this license. Without this expedient, one would be exhausted at the most energetic moment of the phrase.*

*In the example below, if one wishes to draw out the *si blanche*, one is obliged to breathe between the syllables *pre* and *parato* (C).*

Here is an observation of which one will be able to make use in certain cases: if one encounters two consecutive consonants, it will be easy to conceal the inhalation, provided that the second consonant is an explosive. One will take advantage of the preparation of that second consonant in order to breathe through the nose. Examples:

*Rossini: *Gazza ladra*, Cavatina.

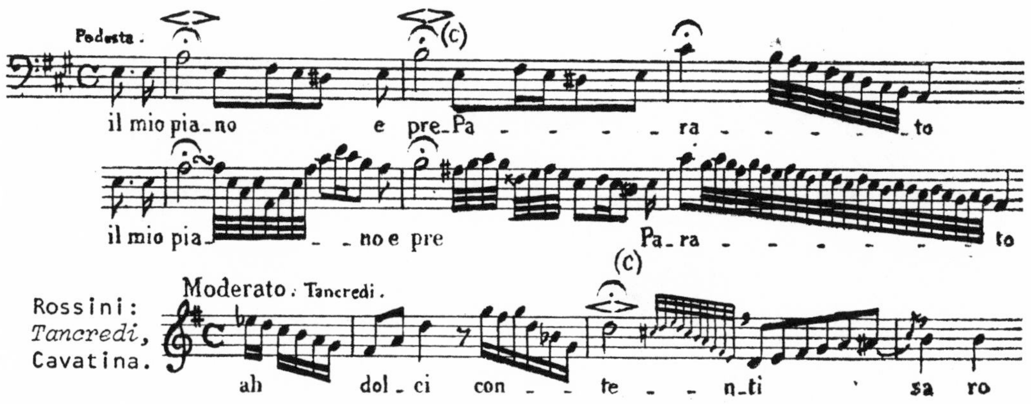

When after a long sustained note one encounters a pause, one should take advantage of the noise of the accompaniment in order to breathe. Example:

Time.

"*Il tempo è l'anima della musica*," says Anna-Maria Celloni.[40] Time, by the regularity of its progress, gives the music steadiness and cohesion; its irregularities lend the performance variety and interest. The time is correct when one fulfils the entire value of the pauses as well as that of the notes. This exactitude introduces self-assurance

---

[40] *Grammatica, o siano regole di ben cantare*, Rome.

into the movement, a very important quality, and one which few artists possess.

In order to define the measure clearly, it is necessary to attack its strong beats, especially its first beat, by an inflection. [E] It is in this manner that one brings out the final cadences in pieces ended with ardor. One can cite as examples:

The allegro of the trio from *Guillaume Tell*, "Embrassons-nous,"

The allegro of the duet from *Otello*, "L'ira d'avvarso fato,"

The stretta from the finale of *Otello*,

The stretta from the finale of *Don Giovanni*.

In such a case, the voice produces the effect of a percussion instrument, and proceeds in like manner striking detached beats.[41]

Considered in its progress, time is presented under three different aspects; it is regular, free or mixed.

1. The time must be regular when the tune includes a very decided rhythm. Such a rhythm, we have said, is generally composed of notes of short value. The songs of war, the outbursts of enthusiasm, especially demand a very accented and regular time. Examples:

Allegro. Figaro.
Mozart:
Nozze di Figaro,
Aria.
Non piu audrai farfal_lo neamo_ro_so
*Rossini:
Gazza ladra,
Duet.
oh cielo ren_dimi al caro ben ohscagliaunfalmmeche mardailsen

---

[41]This attack is operated by means of the *coup de glotte* or by a stress on the consonant, according to whether the word begins with a vowel or a consonant. If one would strike these notes softly, one would destroy the periodic element, and therefore the rhythm itself.

The compositions of Haydn, Mozart, Cimarosa, Rossini, etc., require a complete exactness in the rhythmic movement. Every change made in the values must, without altering the movement of the measure, result from the use of the *tempo rubato*.

2. The time is free when it follows, like speech, the movements of the emotion and the accents of prosody; plainsong and recitatives are examples of free time.

3. Finally, the time is mixed when the expression of the piece produces frequent irregularities in the general movement; this is what one often recognizes in the manifestation of tender and sad feelings. Usually, in these pieces, the value of the notes is long, and the rhythm little felt. The singer should then avoid accenting the time too much and giving it a character of regularity or stiffness. Example:

The irregularities of time are the *rallentando*, the *accelerando*, the *ad libitum*, *a piacere*, *col canto*, etc.

The Rallentando.

The rallentando expresses the decrease of the emotion and consists in slowing the tempo in all parts at the same time, so as to give more charm and grace to certain passages. One uses it at the returns of certain motives. Examples:

*Meyerbeer: *Robert le diable*, Duet.

Rossini: *Guillaume Tell*, Duet.

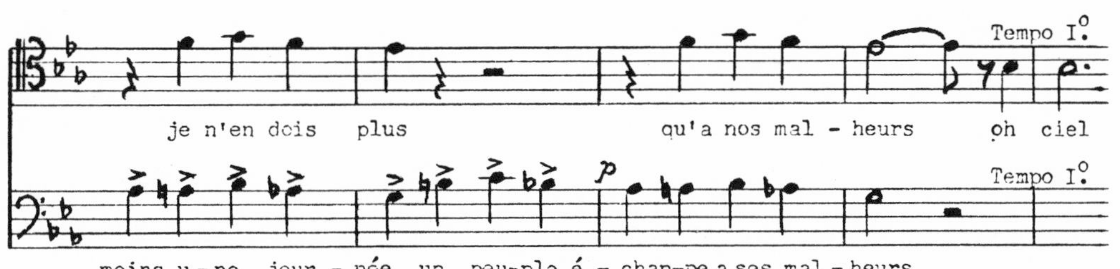

The Accelerando.

The *accelerando* is the opposite of the *rallentando*. It hurries the tempo more and more to enliven the effect.[42]

The Ad Libitum.

In *ad libitum* phrases one *always* slows the tempo. But this kind of free motion is not at all introduced arbitrarily. When the singer believes he should risk such prolongations, he will not at all slow the

---

[42]In the quintet from *Beatrice di Tenda* the final forty-four measures progress with a constant increase of tempo.

The music of Donizetti and especially that of Bellini includes a great number of passages which, without carrying the indication of the rallentando or the accelerando, call for the use of them.

We often reproduce the same examples; but each time they serve to explain a different principle; all of which proves that the performance of the most simple passage requires, in order to be complete, the cooperation of very different means, and often the application of all the precepts of the art.

tempo as a whole, but he will have recourse to the *tempo rubato*, of which we will speak in a moment.

Certain pieces present by turns a nearly free fragment in the voice and a strictly rhythmic fragment in the accompaniment. Example: *Rossini: *Donna del lago*, Aria. [F]

The suspensions and the pauses completely stop the accompaniment, and for a few moments leave a complete independence to the singer.

Tempo Rubato.

The momentary prolongation of value which one gives to one or to several tones to the detriment of others is called *tempo rubato*.

This distribution of the values by lengthening and shortening certain notes, at the same time as it serves to break the monotony of equal movements, is favorable to outbursts of passion. Examples:

In order to make the effect of the tempo rubato perceptible in singing, it is necessary to sustain the tempo of the accompaniment with precision. The singer, free on this condition to increase and decrease alternately the partial values, will be able to set off certain phrases in a new way. The accelerando and the rallentando require that the accompaniment and the voice move together and slow down or speed up the movement as a whole. The tempo rubato, on the contrary, accords this liberty only to the voice. One thus commits a grave fault when, in order to render warmly the very animated cadences of the duet from the *Barber*, one suddenly uses the ritardando in place of the tempo rubato in the next-to-the-last measure, as for example at (A) below: [G]

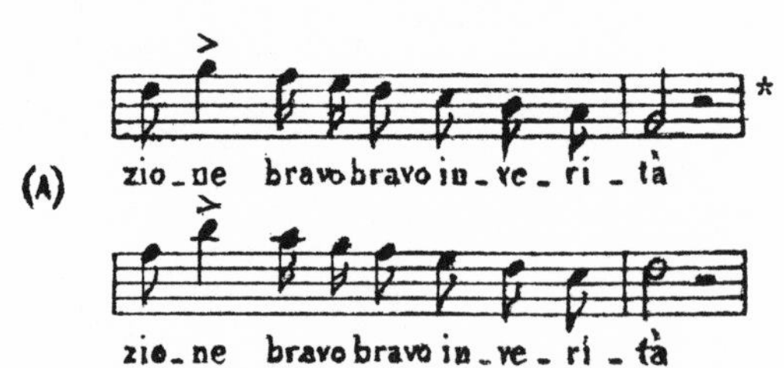

By the first means, while looking for enthusiasm, one falls into awkwardness and sluggishness.

One gives this prolongation[43] to appoggiaturas, to notes which carry the long syllable, to notes *naturally important* [saillantes] *to the harmony*, or to those which one wants to make stand out. In all

---

[43]The prolongation [*temps d'arrêt*], Part One, is the first element of the tempo rubato.

these cases, one makes up the lost time by accellerating the other notes. It is one of the best means of giving color to melodies. Examples:

Donizetti: *Lucia*, Cavatina.

Donizetti: *Anna Bolena*, Cavatina.

Two artists of a very different kind, Garcia (my father), and Paganini, excelled in the use of the tempo rubato applied *by phrase*. While the orchestra maintained the tempo regularly, they, on their part, abandoned themselves to their inspiration to rejoin with the bass only at the moment the harmony would change, or else at the very end of the phrase. But this means requires before everything an exquisite feeling of the *rhythm* and an imperturbable poise. One can scarcely use such a procedure except in passages where the harmony is stable, or slightly varied. Outside of these exceptions it would appear conspicuously harsh to the ear and would present great difficulties to the performer. Here is a use of this difficult means which is always favorable:[44]

---

[44]This example offers the approximate indication of one of the uses which my father made of the tempo rubato.

Rossini: *Il Barbiere di Siviglia*, Duet.

The tempo rubato is also useful in another connection; it facilitates the preparation of the trill by permitting the taking of that preparation on the values which precede. Examples:

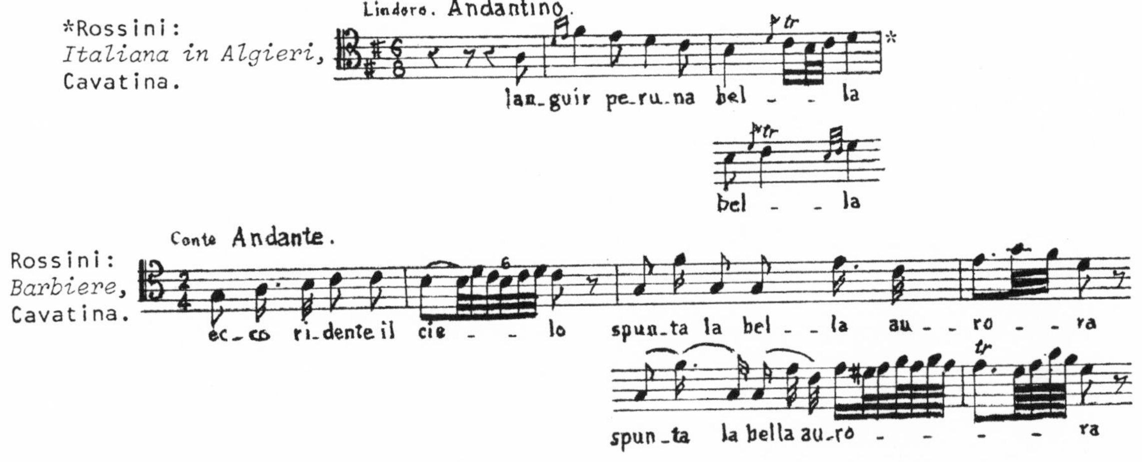

*Rossini: *Italiana in Algieri*, Cavatina.

Rossini: *Barbiere*, Cavatina.

Used without discernment and with affectation, the tempo rubato would have the effect of destroying the balance and distorting [*tourmenter*] the melody.

4. DYNAMICS

Inflections or Accents.

Dynamics, considered as modulating isolated notes, is called *inflection* [translator's italics]. For this word, one generally substitutes that of *accent*, which is then limited in its acceptance to having a very special meaning.

The most regular accents of sung melody have as their basis the accents of spoken language and fall on the stroke of the strong beat of the measure and on the long syllables of the words. But as that disposition of the accents would not suffice to characterize the various kinds of rhythm, the accents are not placed exclusively on the strong beats; they can carry equally well on the stroke of the strong beats, or on that of the weak beats. Examples:

Sometimes the accent even carries uniquely on the weak beat, or on the weak half of the strong beat, and displaces the tonic accent. Syncopation and off-beats [*contre-temps*] are examples of this. [H]

Syncopation.

One always places the accent on the syncopations, and this accent should always be executed from the strong to the weak, and not like echos, which follow the opposite procedure. Examples:

Rossini: *Italiana in Algieri*, Duet.

In order to produce the effect of the off-beat [*contre-temps*], one places the inflection exclusively on the weak beats, or on the weak half of the strong beats. This procedure momentarily breaks the regularity of the rhythm and makes the effect more pointed.[45] Examples:

---

[45]The Spanish, much more often than the Italians, have recourse

An accent is also placed on *appoggiaturas*, and on dotted notes.

Example:

B
Pacini:
Niobe,
Aria.
i tuoi fre_quen_ti pal_pi_ti deh fre_na o co_re a_man_te

And on the first note of any motive which is repeated. Examples:

Meyerbeer:
Crociato,
Cavatina.
ah fi_glio_an zioso il cor il cor t'at_tende
*Rossini:
Gazza ladra,
Trio.
Ninetta.
tradi_tor per voi non sento che dis prezzo rabbia or_ror
*

An accent is moreover placed by preference on notes which form intervals which are difficult to grasp, on *dissonances*, for example; in this case, one accompanies the accent by the prolongation, or else, according to the musical taste, one places the accent on one note or another which one may choose in passages of equal notes. One consults only the need to escape uniformity. Examples:

Rossini:
Quartet.
cielo il mio labbroins pi - - - - ra
Rossini:
Barbiere,
Duet.
Rosina.
ah tu so_ _lo amor tu se_ _i

---

to this liberty in their popular songs; and although the Spanish language has a prosody as accentuated as the Italian language, the popular songs nearly always regulate the accent of the words according to the need of the music. This liberty is actually one of the characteristics which most especially distinguishes their national music, and I do not know if it is met in the same degree in the music of any other country.

One can notice that the accent and the prolongation follow approximately the same laws.

The influence of *dynamics* in general embraces a phrase in its entirety.

The Portamento.

The portamento is a means, by turns energetic or gracious, to color the melody. Applied to the expression of vigorous feelings, it should be strong, full and rapid. Examples:

Used in tender and gracious movements, it will be slower and more gentle. Examples:

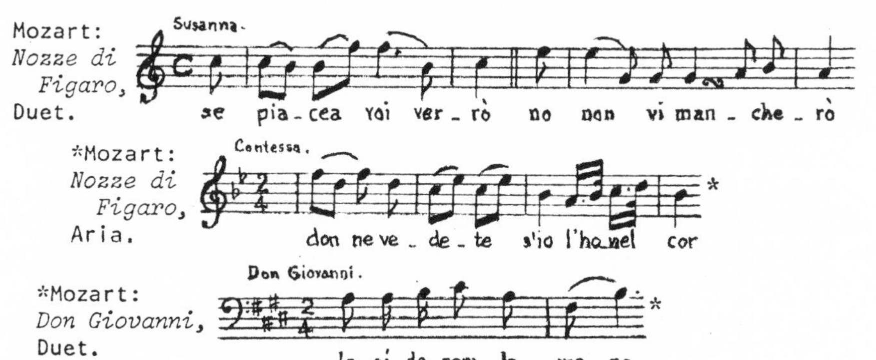

Bellini: *Norma*, Cavatina.

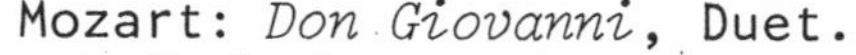

Mozart: *Don Giovanni*, Duet.

*Rossini: *Il Barbiere di Siviglia*, Cavatina.

*Rossini: *Cenerentola*, Duet.

*Mozart: *Don Giovanni*, Aria.

*Rossini: *Semiramide*, Aria.

*Cimarosa: *Sacrifizio d'Abraham*, Aria.

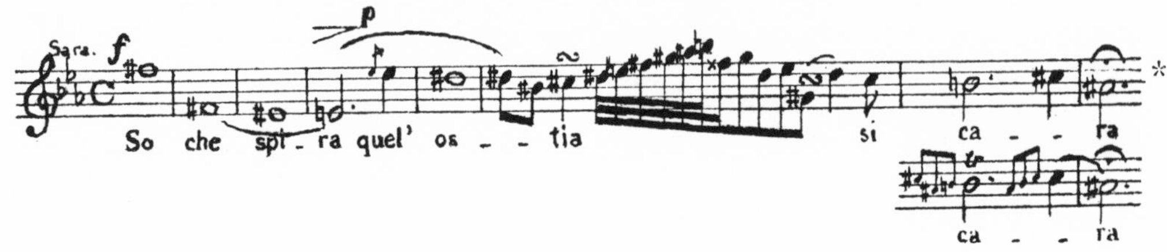

The portamento is performed by leading the syllable which one is going to leave, and not as it is too often done in France, with the following syllable taken by anticipation. [J] One should even hear the note which corresponds to the second syllable an instant early; but one articulates that syllable only at the moment when the value indicated by the note begins. Example:

Cimarosa: *Sacrifizio d'Abraham*, Aria.

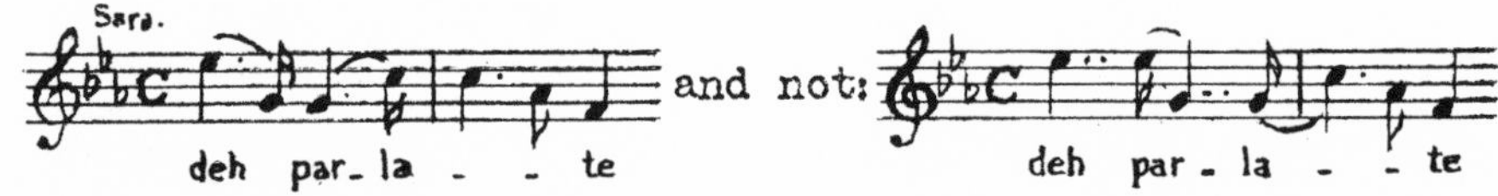

The circumstances in which it is fitting to use the portamento are difficult to define precisely and could scarcely be determined in a precise manner by means of general rules. One can say however that the portamento will be appropriate anytime when, in impassioned language, the voice would move under the impression of an energetic or tender feeling. Omit the portamento in Mozart's phrase: "*E sposa in me*," and the tender expression would disappear.

But this means, for the very reason of its effectiveness, should be used only with reservation; by being lavish with it, one would risk making the performance weak and listless.

Some singers, whether by negligence, or by lack of taste, are not content to multiply the portamentos; they commit the fault of adapting them to all the notes under the form of an inferior dragging, by placing, as we have just said, on that dragging, the second syllable by anticipation. That method has the result of destroying the striking of the second note, and the rhythm itself; the song thus weakened becomes a nauseous languor.

In the following example, we see this procedure spoil a happy inspiration:

Mayerbeer: *Robert le diable*, Air.

The facility of this manner unfortunately tempts the pupils. As it pains them to syllabicate on the high notes, they place the syllable on the lower note and rise to the high note with the help of the portamento. There exists another procedure which presents the same advantages without exposing the same inconveniences. It suffices to change that inferior dragging into a regular portamento, or else to use little lower notes. Example:

These two means are a resource offered to the voice of limited range in passages which are too high. (They have been spoken of on pages 45 and 46. See: *Distribution of the Words under the Notes*.)

We should also call to the attention of the singer another fault no less serious in the execution of the portamento. It is a kind of miauling which does not fail to be produced when, while carrying the voice over some high notes, one drags the voice while opening the timbre. In order to overcome this fault, it is necessary to give a little more movement to the portamento in the high part than in the low part, and especially to cover the timbre, but with precaution and keeping a strong time [*mesure*].

Messa di Voce (*Sons Filés*).

We have spoken, in the first part, of the different kinds of *messa di voce*. See, for the use which one should make of it: *The Canto Spianato*.

Tied Sounds (*Sons liés*).

See: *Breadth or Holding of the Voice on the Words.* (Chapter One, section six.)

Staccato Sounds (*Sons piqués*).

The staccato sounds should be formed, pure and velvety, like those of the harmonica. They especially lend themselves to the expression of touching or gracious feelings. Examples: [K]

*Rossini: *Il Barbiere di Siviglia*, Cavatina.

When one imparts to the sounds the prolongation and the reinforcement (which has been spoken of in Part One, in the discussion of staccato notes), but without detaching the notes, one produces a certain undulation, or echo, which gives the phrase the effect of indecision and tenderness. This means especially suits high notes, and serves to correct their natural thinness. Example:

Bellini: *Pirata*, Aria.

Detached Sounds (*Staccati*).

In general, this accent is not brought out with enough precision. It consists of leaving the note as soon as it has been attacked. The intonation must be of the greatest exactness and the sounds perfectly clear so they can be perceived in an instant. Examples:

*Meyerbeer: *Crociato*, Trio.

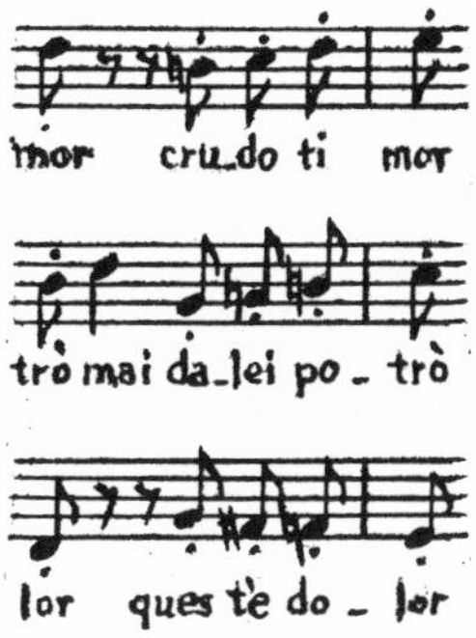

mor cru_do ti mor
trò mai da_lei po_trò
lor ques tè do_lor

Ibid.

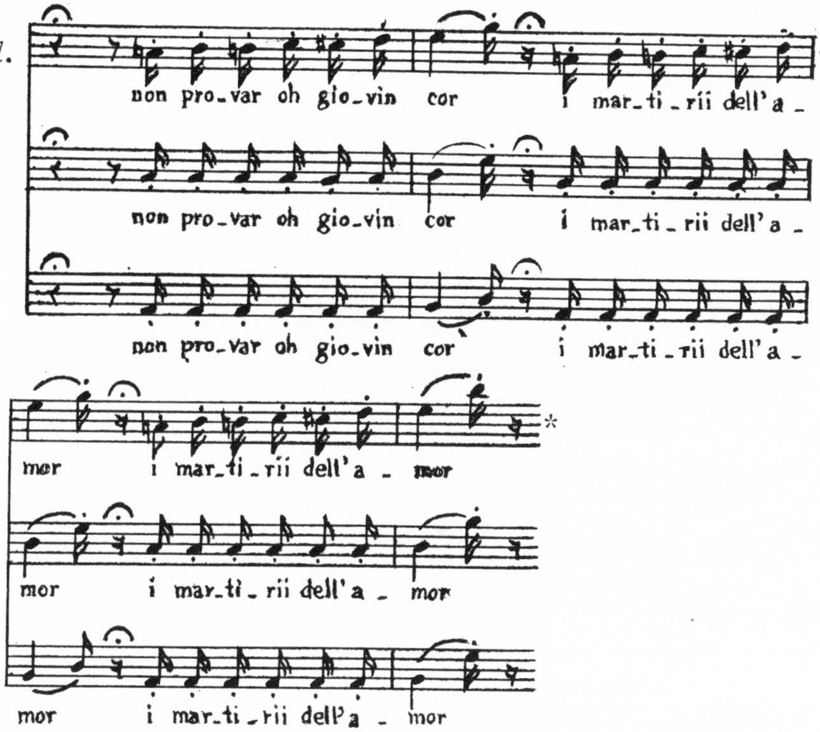

non pro_var oh gio_vin cor i mar_ti_rii dell'a_
non pro_var oh gio_vin cor i mar_ti_rii dell'a_
non pro_var oh gio_vin cor i mar_ti_rii dell'a_
mor i mar_ti_rii dell'a_mor
mor i mar_ti_rii dell'a_mor
mor i mar_ti_rii dell'a_mor
*

Marcato Sounds (*Sons marqués*).

Marcato sounds suit all voices, but especially the basso profundos. Example:

Rossini: *Semiramide*, Trio.

Andante maestoso.
a quei det-tia quel as-pet-to fre - mer sen -
to il cor nel pet-to fre-mer cen-to il cor nel
pet-to ce - - lo a sten - to il lui o ter - ror

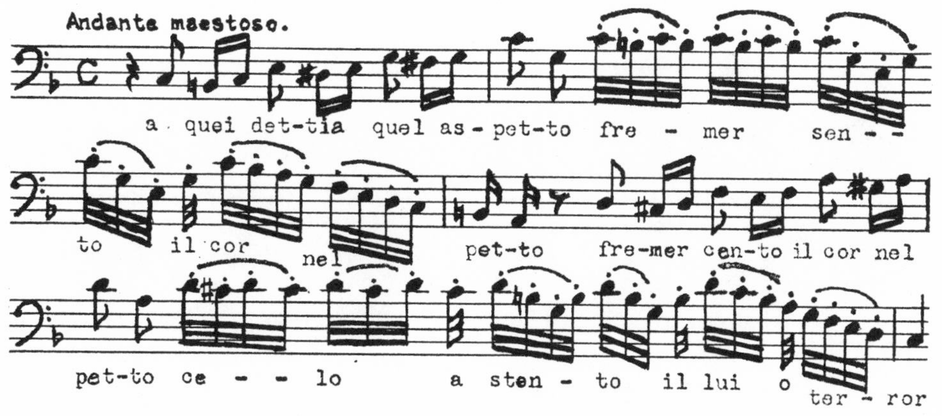

Hammered Sounds (*Sons martelés*).

Hammered sounds seem to me to have a good effect only in silvery and nimble [*deliées*] voices; I would advise the use of them only in the women's voices. Example:

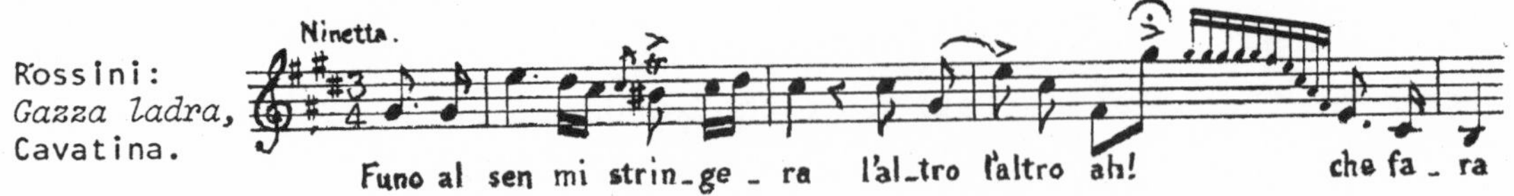

Dotted Notes (*Notes pointées*).

In motives formed by dotted notes, and of as pronounced a character as the following examples,

one should allot a vowel and the *sforzando* to the short notes as well as to the long ones. This procedure makes the short note more meaningful, and saves for it, in spite of its shortness, all the importance which it should have. [L] As much as we believe it necessary to thrust [*pointer*] the above examples and others of the same kind, so much we would reprimand the habit which would incline one to dot notes of equal value.

One would spoil the following melody if one would alter in the least the equality of the values.

*Mozart:
Nozze di Figaro,
Aria.

In this kind of singing, the measure should be felt, but not marked. Moreover, the meaning of the words, more yet than the written values, should determine the choice of accentuation. Motive 1. would be weakened as to the accentuation at the words: "Oui, vous l'arracher..." if it were performed as shown in example 2; whereas it would have to be marked firmly if one placed there the words: "Retournez..." See example 3.

*Rossini:
Guillaume Tell,
Duet.

Dynamics in General (*Forte-piano d'ensemble*).

After having examined cursorily the partial accents which one can impart to the details of the melody, let us examine what the general shades are which the various thoughts can receive.

Dynamics, applied to different joined notes, can include from motives to complete periods; that is to say every musical thought, from the shortest to the most extensive.

Dynamics offers the elementary varieties which follow:

Uniform intensity

The *crescendo*

The *diminuendo*

The *crescendo* followed by the *diminuendo*

The *diminuendo* followed by the *crescendo*

Finally, the uniform intensity broken by

inflections.

One will be able, for example, to utter a first phrase in one of the shades indicated above. The second phrase will receive the same shade, or else a different shade which will be appropriate to it, and so on. This progression, applied to each melody in its smallest details, permits the coloring of the phrases, one after the other, and giving them all the variety which their interest requires. The following examples will clarify our thought:

Period of equal intensity, piano:

Phrase of equal intensity, forte:

Two phrases, one crescendo, the other diminuendo:

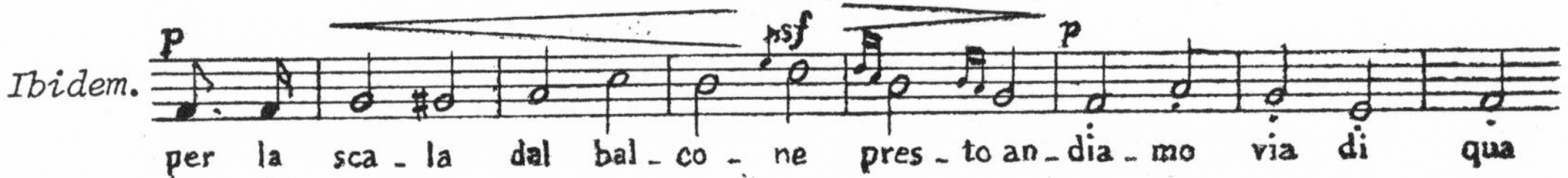

Phrase of equal intensity, piano:

Phrase changing from forte to piano:

Phrases which join the various combinations:

Two phrase members, one piano, the other forte:

Two motives, one strong, the other weak:

Two motives, one cresc., the other dimin.:

Ibidem.

cresc. f

di ques - - to non v'ha

Period which combines various cases:

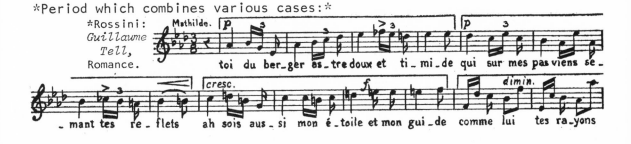

*Rossini: *Guillaume Tell*, Romance.

Mathilde. p p

toi du ber-ger as - tre doux et ti - mi - de qui sur mes pas viens se - mant tes re - flets ah sois aus - si mon é - toile et mon gui - de comme lui tes ra - yons

cresc. f dimin.

cresc.
mf
dim.
tes ra_yons sont dis_crets et l'é _ cho seu_le _ ment re_di_ra mes se_crets re _
_ di _ _ ra mes se _ _ crets mes se _ crets

In a great number of these cases, the applications of the chiaroscuro should be abandoned to the inspirations of the feeling. Other times, on the contrary, one can make use of certain considerations, and determine with certitude the colors which the phrases or the portions of the phrases should receive.

In general, the composer replies to one portion of a phrase with another portion of equal length, composed of identical values, or of different values. Let us observe here that it is by the identical values, more than by the intervals, that the correlation of the musical ideas is established. This observation will serve as a basis for the considerations which we are going to present. If this common bond between the phrases and the members of the phrases, the *equality of value*, did not exist, the thoughts would be distinct; they would be able to connect with each other, but not derive from each other by a strict law of filiation which submits them to a provided for and determined coloring. Also, in what we have to say, we will assume the equality of values between the portions of the melody which we want to compare.

When the second member of the phrase is composed of the same values as the first, the color of the second member is determined by that of the first only if the intervals proceed by melodic progressions, or else when the intervals of the first member are produced in the second.

Any other disposition in the intervals would not imply any necessary dependence between the colors of the two members. Examples:

The second portion of the thought is of the same order as the first; it serves to complete it, but it is entirely independent of it as to effect.

But when the second part is equal to the first in values and in intervals, one can establish in advance that it will be necessary to use in the second part, either the tempo rubato, *as shown in example 1,* or the contrast of effect, *as shown in example 2,* and to oppose between them the *piano* and the *forte*. *The members of the phrase: *Più fiero martire* and *mi venga a consolar*, can again serve as an example. The first motive is forte, the second is piano.*

When the thought is repeated identically several times in succession,[46] or when the thought follows an ascending or descending sequence,

[46] These repetitions are frequent with all composers, but especially with Mozart.

it is necessary, following the feeling of the phrase, to submit these diverse developments to the *crescendo* or the *diminuendo*, to the *accellerando* or the *ritardando*, more rarely to the isolated accents or to the *tempo rubato*.

The *forte* should answer the *forte* in energetic feelings; in gracious feelings, on the contrary, it is the *piano* which answers the *forte*. Every transition from one degree of force to a different degree of force produces a perceptible effect. The *forte* succeeding the *piano* strikes the ear, the same as the *piano* replacing the *forte*; only, when it is the *pianissimo* which ends the phrase, it is necessary to separate it from the forte by a slight pause, striking the note an instant after the bass, as indicated in the following example:

Attack the C after the bass.

This silence rests the ear from the loud notes, and prepares it to grasp even the most delicate effects which may follow; but that is especially the case when one takes care to strike clearly the first consonant presented after the silence.

With the exception of the preceding cases, the *forte*, the *piano*, the *crescendo* and the *diminuendo* are used only according to the feeling, and not for reasons of musical form. As a consequence, the forms which arise can receive the *rinforzando* if the feeling becomes animated, and the *diminuendo* if the feeling softens. It is the same for the descending forms. *Here are some examples in which the melodic form receives the *crescendo* and the *diminuendo*, not for reasons of the direction of the passage, but of the expression which it should take.*

The rule stated in some works, and which prescribes always applying the *crescendo* to ascending forms and the *diminuendo* to descending forms, thus governs only certain particular cases, and should not be posed as a general principle.

One can, as we have seen, color the music as a whole, or in its details. In order to color on a broad scale [*d'une manière large*], one imparts to each phrase an even degree of strength, a single timbre, a unique effect. One phrases then by phrases and by periods, taking care only that these periods not be too long. This manner of shading is very theatrical, and only suits thoughts which are unfolded slowly.

In order to color in detail, one applies oneself to making clear all the finesses of the melodic ideas. Each motive in particular, each intention should have its effect. This manner portrays better the movements of lively and short ideas, and suits both the gracious and the comic styles. It is applied with equal success to salon pieces and to the theater.

If one wishes that the nuances of the dynamics produce some effect, one should, in general, maintain a natural and very equal diction. It is an error common to several artists to believe that ability consists in giving all parts of the performance indiscriminately an extreme vigor. When everything is energetic, the energy is actually perceived nowhere. In general, the source of the most characterized effects is in the variety and the *contrast* of the intentions. *It is by preparing one effect by the contrary effect* that one obtains the most brilliant effects; for example, a *forte* will stand out only in the condition of being preceded by a *piano*. A passage composed of rapid notes will have to come after several sustained notes, etc., etc.

5. BEGINNINGS--SUSPENSIONS--REPRISES--ENDINGS OF PHRASES

The free and unhampered pace of the diction depends to a great extent upon the manner of beginning, suspending, and connecting the various members of a melody.

Beginnings.

The beginning of the discourse [*entrée en matière*] should be neither abrupt nor shocking. The ear and the feeling require that the introduction, while keeping much freedom, be first calm and restrained. The changes will bring about by degrees the development of the warmth which the piece requires. The most energetic efforts displease when they are produced by jerks. This observation applies not only to the attack of a song, but also to that of the particular tones. Even when these are meant to receive a great intensity, one should prepare them by a *reinforcement* [*un renfort*]. This precaution is especially necessary for the high notes, which one cannot force without making the voice lose its harmony and without imparting to it the dryness of the scream [*cri*].

Suspensions and reprises.

When a song has been suspended by a momentary rest one resumes it in the same degree of strength and in the same timbre as before the interruption. Thus, the endings of the *conduits*[47] should be slowed and softened by degrees every time the melody expresses a sweet feeling. Here are some examples which are frequently encountered: [M]

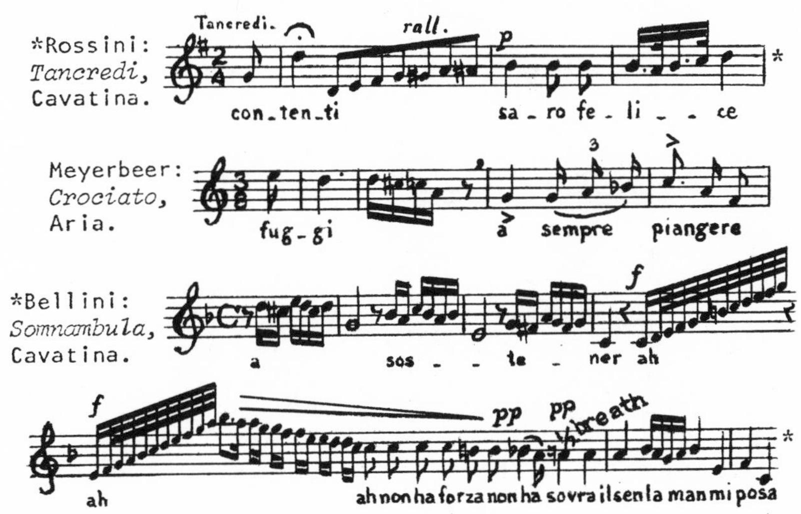

In these three phrases, one should slow down, soften, and gradually carry the voice up to the first note of the motive. [N] *The first two examples present a particular difficulty: one does not know where to take his breath. It is necessary first to execute the portamento between the a and the b, the a and the g; then, the note scarcely touched, to inhale quickly and delicately, and finally to take the b or the g very softly, as one had just left it. This *half breath* should not be suspected by the listener.*

This kind of passage changes character entirely for energetic sentiments. In the following examples, the *conduit* should be vigorous:

---

[47]A particular kind of passage [*point d'orgue*] which serves to bring back the motive.

In all these examples of pauses [*points d'orgue*], of *conduits*, or of resuming the tempo after a phrase *a piacere*, one indicates, by means of a consonant, the precise moment when the accompaniment should begin again.[48] The singer should finish the phrase slowly, hold for its full value the long vowel which precedes the *resolving* consonant, and to make especially understood by a prolonged preparation, the moment when this strikes *in tempo*.

The phrase which would resume the *a tempo* abruptly without giving notice of the instant of the attack, as for example:

Donizetti: *Torquato Tasso*, Aria. [O]

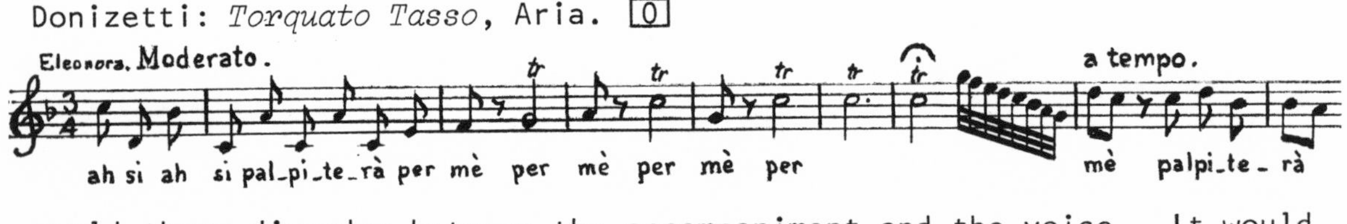

would throw disorder between the accompaniment and the voice. It would be necessary to give it an ending which might indicate the moment of the

[48]See *Consonants*.

reprise, as for example:

Endings.

The manner in which the motives, the members of the phrases, the phrases, the periods, the pieces [*morceaux*] are ended merits all our attention. The various rests of the melody are indicated by means of a silence which follows the final note of the phrases or of the portions of the phrases. As a consequence, that note, in the motives, members of phrases, or phrases, should be left lightly and instantaneously. If one would prolong that last note too much, the thought would lose its articulations and would cease to be elegant.[49]

In the slow movements, such as the *cantabile* and *largo* sections, etc., these same final notes take more length; but that length is always proportional to the values which precede it and the rest which follows it.

The note which ends the final period, cadenza-like passages [*points d'orgue*], *accompanied* recitatives, should be longer than all the other final notes, for it indicates the conclusion of the thought or

[49]The prolongation of these final notes would make the singing heavy and would absorb a part of the time necessary to renew the breath. This unfortunate prolongation is vulgarly called a *tail*. It is also necessary to carefully avoid rushing this last note in order to take a new breath more quickly, and as a consequence [*à la suite*] to give up the air which the chest could contain. In this case one would produce a groan; in the preceding, a jerk.

that of the discourse. Let us add that these final notes will be louder in masculine words [*tronchi*] than in feminine words [*piani*], and longer in *serious* music than in *comic* music. Examples:

The end of the phrase should always be maintained in the sentiment of the phrase, that is to say that that ending will be soft, medium or loud, only in proportion with the expression of the melody, and not always loud as a stereotype, or always soft for a lack of vigor, as one can often observe with some singers.

In the bodies of the phrases, it is necessary to avoid falling heavily on notes which require a resolution. Examples:

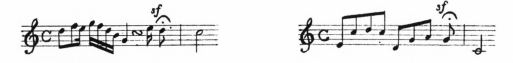

This accent is too lively [*vif*] to be wasted, even at the ends of cadenzas [*points d'orgue*].

In movements with a very accentuated rhythm, the final cadences are the last burst of passion. The vigorous articulation of the time by means of the consonant and the inflection, the appoggiaturas, the ornamentation, the warmth, all combine, in able singers, to give this decisive moment the final degree of the effect.

CHAPTER III

ALTERATIONS

We will concern ourselves in this chapter with the particular devices [*moyens*] which are designated under the name of alterations [*changements*].

One introduces alterations into pieces, either for necessity, or to add to the effect.

The necessity of effecting alterations in the notes can result from diverse causes. Let us suppose a work with a tessitura of which the pitch is too high or too low for the voice of the performer; let us suppose again that the style of the work, whether declamatory or florid, is not in accord with that of the singer; one understands then that the artist must alter the composition at some points: thus, he will lower or raise certain passages, he will simplify them or change them to fit them to his abilities [*moyens*] or to the character of his talent. If it were a question of only an aria or a duet, it would be necessary to transpose them completely rather than displace the essential effects of it. However, whatever ability one may deploy in these arrangements, it is rare that one succeeds in satisfying the composer or the public. It would be more wise for the singer to abandon a work which was not appropriate to the resources of his talent than to expose himself by forcing his means, offending accepted traditions, and perverting distinguished works.

Let us pass to the alterations motivated by the need to introduce new effects. When the accent is not at all sufficient to color the melody in some of its parts or in its entirety, one has recourse to the use of ornaments [*fioritures*], which receive the nuances described in the preceding chapters. Nearly all the Italian music composed before the nineteenth century is included in this case. The composers, in tracing their idea, would rely upon the accent and the accessories which the talent of the singer could add to it. There are different kinds of pieces which, because of their nature, are confided to the free and capable inspiration of the performer; such are the variations, rondos, polkas [*polacca*], etc. *As the study of ornaments requires much practice, and so it may lead the artist to the improvising of variants [*cantar alla mente*], the distinctive merit of an eminent singer, the teacher could not exercise the student too much in varying the pieces himself.*

*It is good for the student to do many exercises of this kind and try several variations, several different versions [*traits*] of the same passage; in this manner, the critical observations of the teacher will bring more benefit. Besides, what one should desire, especially in a young singer, is fruitfulness, the accuracy will come later; it will be the natural fruit of the lessons and of experience. In the work which we advise, the corrections of the teacher should at the same time make the faults disappear and keep, as much as possible, the intentions of the young composer. The most instructive criticism is that which changes a work without destroying it.*

Moreover, before developing the precepts relative to the ornaments, let us say that the student who has become an artist should use them only when it is appropriate, and with moderation [*sobriété*]. Let us add that, from the moment one begins these exercises, some knowledge of harmony becomes indispensable.

As one cannot establish in advance any categories of ornaments [*fioritures*] adapted to the needs of the various sentiments, the student should consider the ornaments, not in themselves, but with respect to the sentiment which they express. This sentiment will derive its character, not only from the choice of the notes and the form of the passages, but rather more from the expression which the singer imparts to them. It is then the particular intention of the words and of the music which one must constantly consult in the search for the ornaments. Those which would paint a grandiose feeling would not suit, for example, the aria of Rosina, etc. A simple discord between the feeling of the piece and that of the ornaments would be sufficient to be considered a fault. Example:

Rossini: *Il Barbiere di Siviglia*, Cavatina.

One can sense well that the manner of the second example is too languorous for the personality of the character. We insist on the need for affinity between the nature of the composition and that of the ornaments, since, without that accord, it is not possible to keep for each composer and each composition the originality which is proper to it.

In general, the ornaments are exclusively reserved for the voice which carries the melody; so it is necessary that the melody remain free, that is to say that it is neither subjected to a harmony which is too restrictive [*serrée*], nor accompanied or doubled by any *obbligato* instrument [*instrument obligé*].

In duets, the two parts can combine their ornaments, but in ensemble pieces written in concerted parts, one should be forbidden even the slightest alteration.

The application of the oranments gives rise to the same observations as that of the dynamics. The process is absolutely parallel. [A] It suffices to place the ornaments there where one perceives the return of the same values and where the coloring can appear insufficient.

The appropriate ornaments always produce much effect when they terminate a member of the phrase. Example:

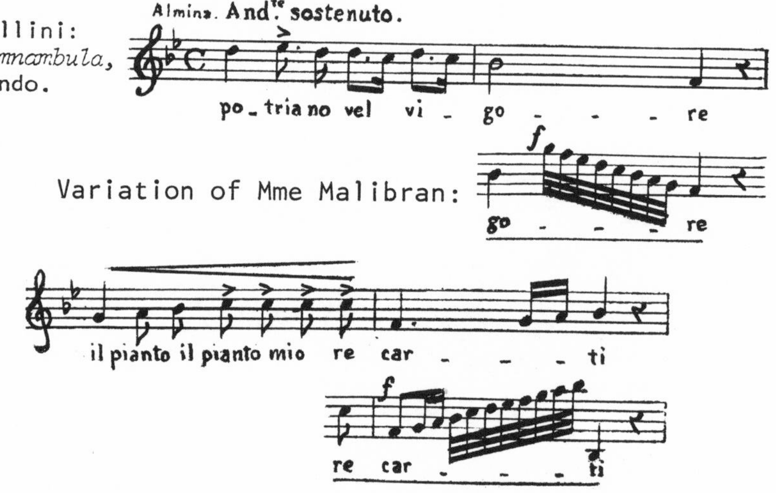

It is because they fall on the weak part of the measure, that which lends itself most naturally to alterations. The ornaments placed thus have the charm of the unforseen and do not alter the melody in its essential part, that is, the notes which fall on the strong beats. These notes, apart from the fact that they make the most of the rhythmic accent, also fulfil very pronounced functions in the harmony; from which it follows that one should modify them with ornaments only with extreme reservation, under the danger of completely perverting the melodic thought.

General rule. One should vary a thought each time it is repeated, whether in its entirety, or in part; that is indispensable both to give a new charm to the thought, and to sustain the attention of the listener.

The pieces which are based upon the return of a motive, the rondos, variations, polkas, the arias and the cavatinas with a second part, are particularly intended to receive ornaments.[50] These alterations, in their disposition, should follow an increasing progression. One first saves his means of effect, and presents the motive in all its simplicity at its exposition; then one mixes into the first repetition some ornaments or accents different from the first; finally, one increases and varies more and more, at each repetition, the ornaments and accents.[51]

---

[50]There are pieces whose motives are so perfect [*heureux*] and so well characterized, that one could not modify it without altering it in an annoying manner. The *Sicilienne* of Pergolesi seems to me to be such a piece.

[51]The following pieces appear to me well chosen for this kind of study:

Cavatina.	"Sovra il sen la man mi posa."	*Sonnambula.*
Rondo.	"Ah non giunge uman pensiero."	*Sonnambula.*
Cavatina.	"Una voce poco fa."	*Barbiere.*
Rondo.	"Nacquî all'affanno."	*Cenerentola.*
Rondo.	"Tanti affetti al cor d'intorno."	*Donna del lago.*
Variations.	"Nel cor più non mi sento."	*La Molinara.*
Aria.	"Dî piacer mi balza il cor."	*Gazza ladra.*
Aria.	"La placida campagna."	*La Principessa in Campagna.*
Aria.	"Jours de mon enfance."	*Pré-aux Clercs.*
Aria.	"Dieu! que viens-je de lire?"	*Ambassadrice.*
Aria.	"Dès l'enfance les mêmes chaînes."	*Serment.*
Aria.	"Voyez-vous là-bas."	*Sirène.*
Aria.	"Ah! je veux briser ma chaîne."	*Diamants de la Couronne.*

This precept of variety, as we have just said, follows the thought in its minutest details. Examples:

The nature of the alterations should correspond to that of the thought of the composer and present the same increase of effect. It is by the brilliancy of the passage or by the number of notes added that one obtains this result. Example:

Rossini: *Il Barbiere di Siviglia*, Duet.

The first passage offers more movement than the second and third, but those prevail by the brilliancy of the intervals.

The rules which precede are confirmed by the example of the better composers themselves, who never reproduce the same thought several times without rejuvenating it by new effects confided to the voices or to the instruments.

But the reproduction of the same values is not the only indication of the need or the appropriateness of ornaments.

If there is reason for painting the sentiment or the thought by imitation, one must not neglect the occasion: one thus pleases the mind and the ear at the same time. The meaning of the words determines, here as elsewhere, the ornaments and the character which the performance demands. Examples:

*Coppola: *Nina*, Cavatina.

Cimarosa:
Matrimonio segreto,
Aria.

Effects of this kind are adapted very well to words which offer images of size, movement, or a harmony imitative of sounds. For example: [B]

Vittoria.	Courage.
Eco.	*S'envole.*
Lampo.	Gloire.
Eterno.	Triomphe.
Guerra, etc.	*Folâtre, etc.*

We can also rank in this category words which express feelings in which our soul complains. *Examples:*

*Donizetti: *Lucia*, Cavatina.

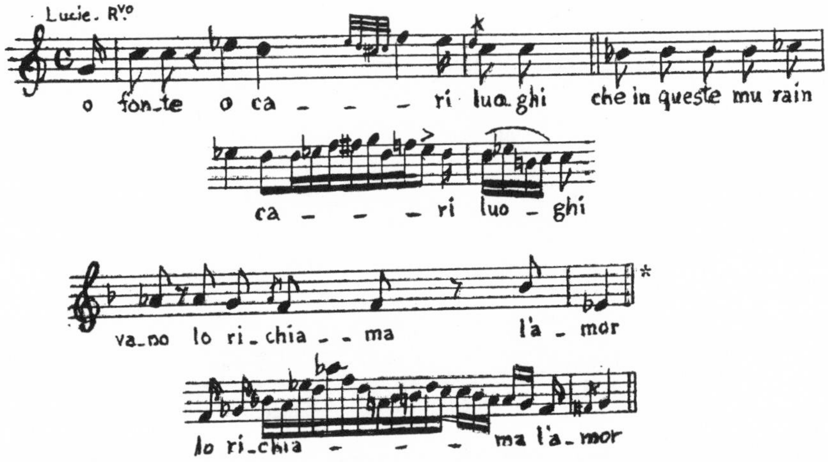

Lucie. R.vo
o fon-te o ca - - - ri luo-ghi che in queste mu rain
ca - - - ri luo - ghi
va-no lo ri-chia - - ma l'a - mor
lo ri-chia - - - ma l'a-mor

*Meyerbeer: *Crociato*, Cavatina.

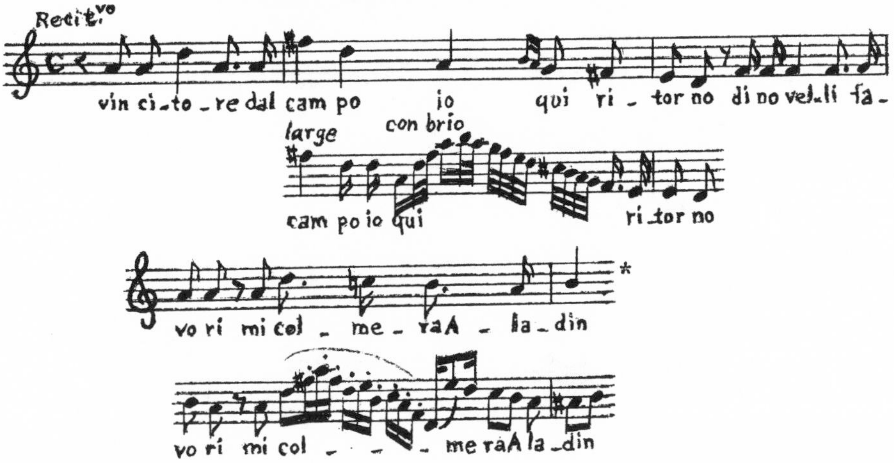

Recit.vo
vin ci-to-re dal cam po io qui ri - tor no di no vel-li fa-
large
con brio
cam po io qui ri-tor no
vo ri mi col - me - ra A - la-din
vo ri mi col - - - me ra A la-din

*Imitation, confined in the limits of taste, presents great beauties, but pushed too far, it degenerates into childishness [*puérilité*].*

One also obtains certain effects of imitation by the particular choice of rhythm or by the value imparted to the notes. Here are some examples:

*Mozart: *Don Giovanni*, Duet.

il cor vam-mion deg-gian do il cor
il cor vam-mion deg-gian do il cor

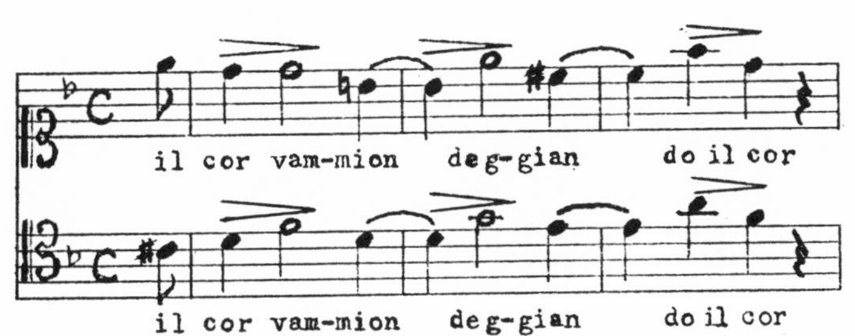

Mozart, in this passage, has expressed by the syncopation the struggle between the diverse feelings.

In the recitative which precedes Nina's aria, one should grant a large value to the following notes, and principally to the last, which it would be well to sustain [*filer*] with some inflections.

In Rosina's cavatina, Mme Malibran would give all the fullness of her voice to the words *mi ri-suo-no*, and the effect of it was astonishing.

Let us add finally the accents imitative of emotion, of which we will speak in the chapter on *Expression*: here, everything is imitation. The ornaments are indispensable in order to fulfil the *conduits* and the cadenza-like passages [*points d'orgue*].

Among the passages [*traits*] of every nature which one can use to decorate the phrases, we will fix our attention principally on the appoggiaturas, the mordents and the trills, because their application is subjected to more precise rules.

1. APPOGGIATURAS (See Part One)

The appoggiatura, as its name indicates, is a note on which the voice marks a stress. [C] This note is almost always non-harmonic and should be resolved to a harmonic note. The harmonists consider only non-harmonic major and minor seconds attacked by conjunct intervals as appoggiaturas; but singers should, I believe, besides these seconds, regard all the intervals which fulfil the same functions, *such as the delayed notes [*retards*] and the disjunct intervals,* as appoggiaturas and subject them to the same rules. [D] *One will be able to distinguish the appoggiaturas into conjunct appoggiaturas and disjunct appoggiaturas.*

In Italian singing, the appoggiatura can scarcely be considered as an ornament, so necessary is it to the prosodic accent. Viewed thus, it is a musical accent which always falls on the strong beats and on the long syllables of the smooth [*piani*] and transitory [*sdruccioli*] words. This circumstance preserves the cadence and melody of the words.[52] [E]

Recitatives as well as measured music offer numerous examples of them.

The appoggiatura can be placed at every interval and receive a long or short value.

---

[52]This rule is applied to all languages. In the singing of French, it is an innovation only for the recitative.

DESCENDING APPOGGIATURAS

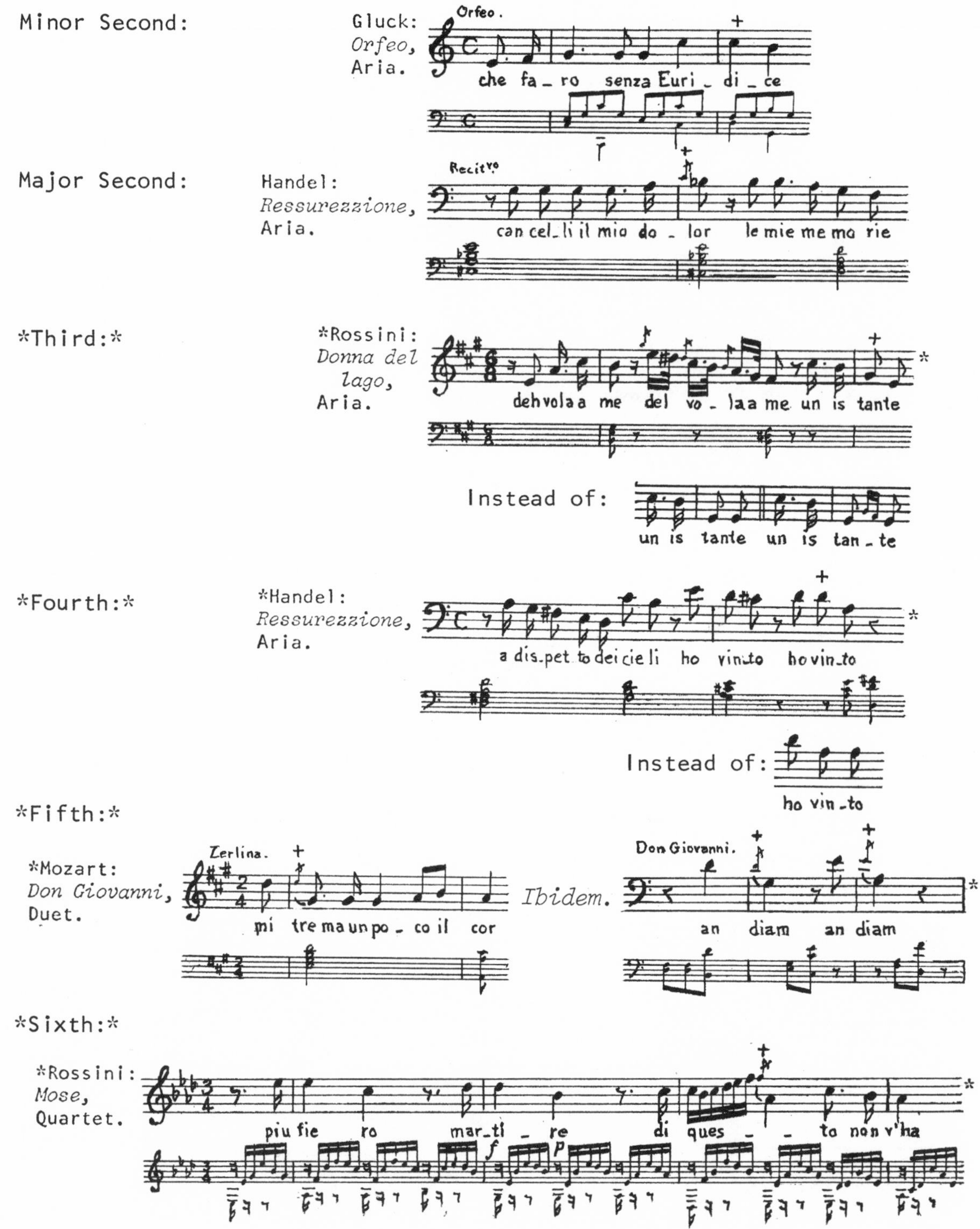

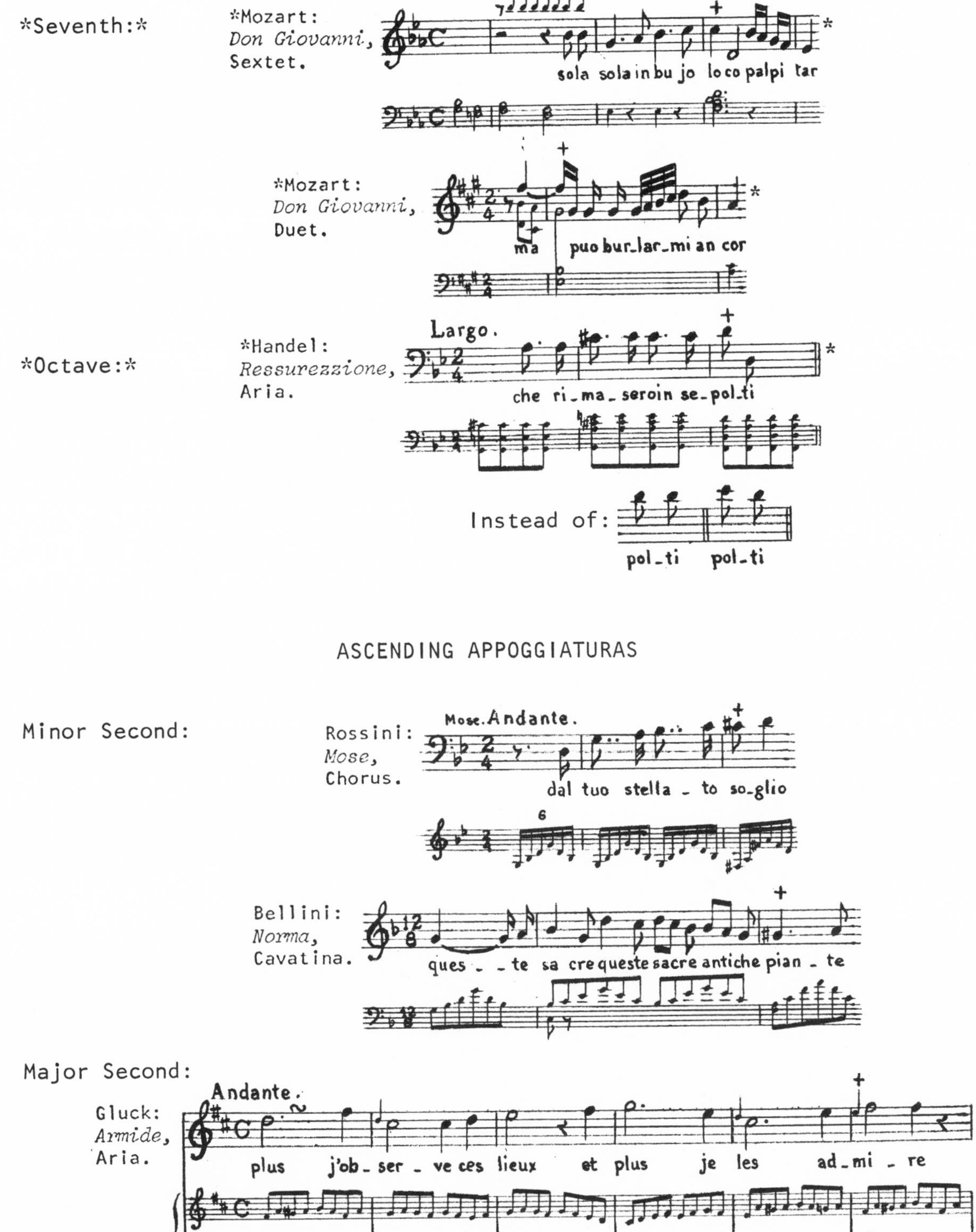
Seventh:
*Mozart:
Don Giovanni,
Sextet.
sola sola in bu jo lo co palpi tar
*Mozart:
Don Giovanni,
Duet.
ma puo bur_lar_mi an cor
Octave:
*Handel:
Ressurezzione,
Aria.
Largo.
che ri_ma_seroin se_pol_ti
Instead of:
pol_ti pol_ti
ASCENDING APPOGGIATURAS
Minor Second:
Rossini:
Mose,
Chorus.
Mose. Andante.
dal tuo stella _ to so_glio
Bellini:
Norma,
Cavatina.
ques _ _te sa cre queste sacre antiche pian _ te
Major Second:
Gluck:
Armide,
Aria.
Andante.
plus j'ob_ser _ ve ces lieux et plus je les ad_mi _ re

Appoggiaturas are written in two manners: in little notes and in ordinary notes. In all the old music with the exception of the recitatives, the appoggiatura was only the simple ornament of one note. It was written in a small character, and one could omit it without disturbing anything in the words; for it had no syllable which belonged to it.

In the recitative, on the contrary, the appoggiatura very often had a specific syllable.

After Mozart and Cimarosa, the appoggiaturas were in many cases written in large notes, and with specific syllables attributed to them.

Their value is determined only in the second case. In the first, their duration changes according to the character of the piece, of the kind of meter and the kind of note to which they belong. [F] *(See part one.)*

Beside the simple appoggiaturas of which we have spoken *up to now,* there are groups of two, three and four appoggiaturas which are added to the real notes or even to the simple appoggiaturas. These groups, according to the number and the disposition of the notes which comprise them, take the names of double or triple appoggiaturas, of *acciaccaturas*, of *mordents* or *grupetti*. They are also designated under the collective name of little notes. (See part one. [G]) Examples:

When the two first notes of the measure end a member of the phrase, the first always carries the prosodic accent, and for this reason it must be changed into an appoggiatura (example A); the effect of the two equal notes (C) would not be tolerable. One should exempt from this rule the cases where the two notes make the essential part of the motive (B). The following phrases can serve as examples:

Pucitta: *Principessa in campagna,* Cavatina.

Handel: *Armide*, Aria.

Sometimes the harmony, whether in ensemble pieces or in solos, does not permit the alteration of the first of the two notes. It is necessary then, in order to break the monotony, to place two or three appoggiaturas between the two sounds. Examples:

Bellini: *Norma,* Duet.

Bellini: *Norma,* Trio.

By bringing together the various ways of varying the two notes followed by a pause with the aid of appoggiaturas, we have the following table:

In place of changing the first note to an appoggiatura, one can conceal [*sauver*] the monotony of the two equal notes by making it, like the second, a harmonic note, but a different chord member. Example: Mozart: *Don Giovanni*, Aria.

But changes of this last kind are more the domain of the composer than of the singer; examples of them are numerous. Often the appoggiatura is followed by different kinds of little notes. Example:

Rossini: *Otello*, Second Finale.

All these precepts can be applied usefully to singing in French.

Acciaccatura (See Part One).

The acciaccatura is used only in descending. Example: [H]

Rossini: *Bianca e Faliero*, Quartet.

Mordent (See Part One).

As we said in the first part, the mordent is placed at the beginning, in the middle or at the end of a tone.

The mordent is used to call attention to a note or a detail, and most often in these forms:

Rhod: *Variations.*

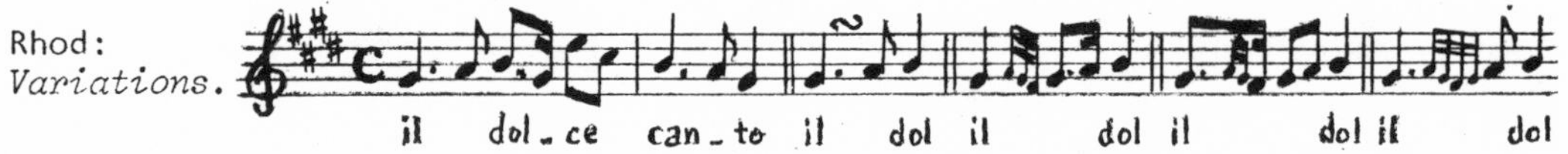

This ornament, the most unspared [*prodigué*] of all, follows the character of the music. It is lively for sentiments which require verve and energy; it is slow [*molle*] in the tender and melancholy sentiments; these modifications it has in common with the trill.[53]

The mordent which does not begin the tone is made after having well placed the note to which it belongs, whether on half of the length of that note, or on the end.[54] Examples:

Mozart
Don Giovanni,
Aria.

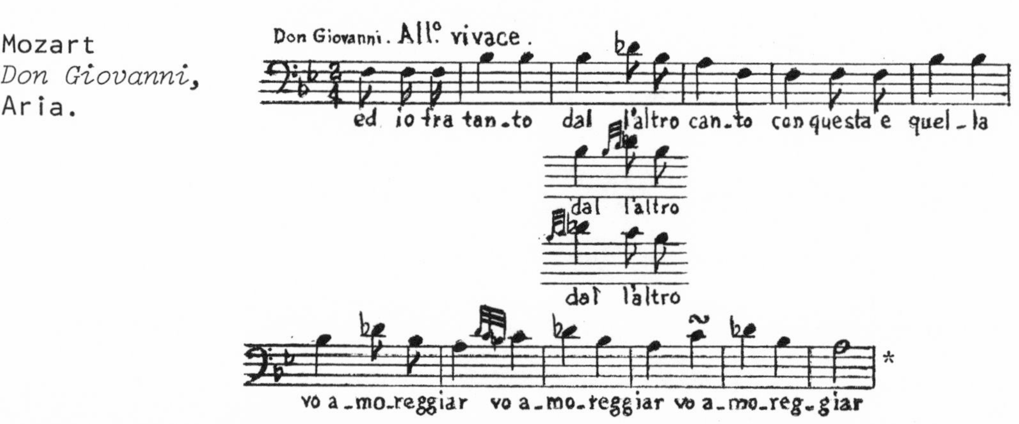

[53] In Spanish songs the notes are attacked suddenly by rapid mordents. Madame Pasta made great use of that manner. It was one of the marked characteristics of her style.

[54] Although the last passage is written in large notes, it should be performed by the movement of the mordent.

2. TRILL (See *Trill*, Part One)

The trill has long been the indispensable termination of the cadence, as the required ending of all vocal pieces. It was especially esteemed in church music.

The trill was always preceded by a longer or shorter, more or less elaborate preparation. It was a preliminary in order to arrive at the beat, and always it ended in a regular manner. Example:

Time has introduced some new customs. One prepares or does not prepare the trill, one stops it suddenly or one adds to it an ending in proportion to the value which one can attribute to it. If it is long, one prepares it and one ends it regularly in all cases. This method is the most elegant. It is practiced by all the good musicians every time the trill is placed on the held notes of cadenza-like passages [*points d'orgue*] and *conduits* or on measured notes of sufficient length. Example:

Rossini: *Armida*, Duet.

Passage sung by G. David.

When the trill is in a sequence by disjunct intervals, one cannot prepare it, but it is well to put endings on all the trills of the sequence. Example:

Rossini: *Gazza ladra*, Cavatina.

If the trill is short, it is not prepared, but it is given an ending. Example:

Mozart: *Don Giovanni*, Aria.

When it is in a diatonic or chromatic sequence, only the first trill is prepared, and only the last is given an ending. All the others are attacked immediately by the auxilliary note and they follow each other without endings. This procedure adds to the energy of the passage all that it makes it lose in elegance. It is thus advisable to apply it to hurried and vigorous movements. The individual preparation and ending in a series of trills would require the slow movement of the *adagio* or the *cantabile*. Examples of trills in diatonic succession:

*Donizetti: *Anna Bolena*, Rondo.

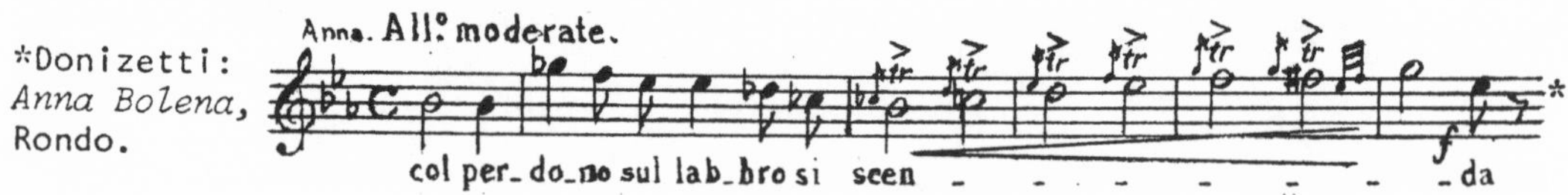

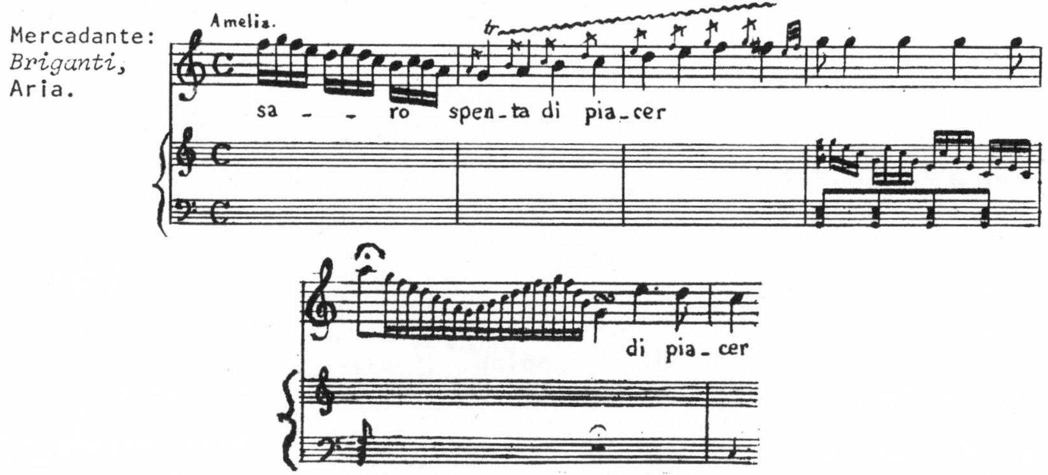

There are, as we have seen, two manners of performing the trill in a chromatic sequence (see Part One), namely: by attacking each trill on each half step, or by trilling a continuous portamento with an equal progression.

Each time that the trill immediately follows a descending scale, one can, without lacking in elegance, omit the preparation. Example:

In the sad sentiments, in order to remove from the trill some of its natural brilliance, which would form a contrast with the general expression of the melody, one does it in measured [*comptées*] notes, not struck by the larynx. It then takes the name of *soft trill*. Example: Zingarelli: *Romeo e Giulietta*, Rondo.

The Doubled Trill (see Part One).

The doubled trill can be placed only on free holds or on notes of long value. Example:

Pucitta: *Principessa in campagna*, Aria.

Performance of the trill mordent:

Performance of the trill mordent:

ritard.

va

la

scher_zan_do va

la

pla_cida campagna

pla_cida campagna

pp

These forms can be used on all the tones of a chord. The following form is reserved for the third, fifth and seventh of the chords composed of these same intervals.

The Trill Mordent (*Ribattuta di gola*, see Part One).

The trill mordent, as we have said, consists in a double stroke of the larynx ended by a mordent. Example:

Rossini: *Otello*, Cavatina.

Otello. All°
per voi dun nuo - vo af - fet - to sen - to sento in - fi - am - mar il cor
Or else:

One sometimes makes a simple stroke [*battuta di gola*]. Example:

Sometimes the mordent is omitted, and the two strokes take the name of *ribattuta*.

Let us observe that the doubled trill, the trill mordent, the *battuta* and the *ribattuta di gola*, the mordent [*tour de gosier*], the acciaccatura, the *martellement* (also so-called the *ribattuta di gola*),[55] are only the different effects presented by the modifications of the *pulsating* or the *trembling* of the throat. These are fragments of the trill, of which some replace each other mutually in order to decorate a note, whether on attacking it, or in the middle of its value, or to end it. The extreme lightness of these ornaments has assured them for all time, just as the appoggiaturas, the privilege of easily finding a place

---

[55]Brossard, *Dictionnaire de Musique*, 1703. The double uses which one can notice in these technical words arise from the lack of precision in the language of the early [*anciens*] authors.

in all styles.

3. *POINT D'ORGUE* { *Arbitrio* / *Fermata* / *Cadenza* }

The *point d'orgue* (organ point) is a suspension of the musical direction which can be maintained only momentarily, or which can take place at a final pause named *perfect cadence*. The *point d'orgue* is indicated by the sign 𝄐 𝄑. The words *point d'orgue* also designate in a wider sense the ornaments which are very often placed there.

The momentary suspensions are principally placed on the two perfect chords, major and minor, on the dominant seventh chord, and on the inversions which furnish the three kinds of chords.

The suspensions which precede a complete rest are placed exclusively on the chords of the $\frac{6}{4}$ followed by the dominant seventh, on this last chord alone, or on the ninths. Examples:

On the $\frac{5}{3}$ chord: Rossini: *Donna del lago*, Rondo.

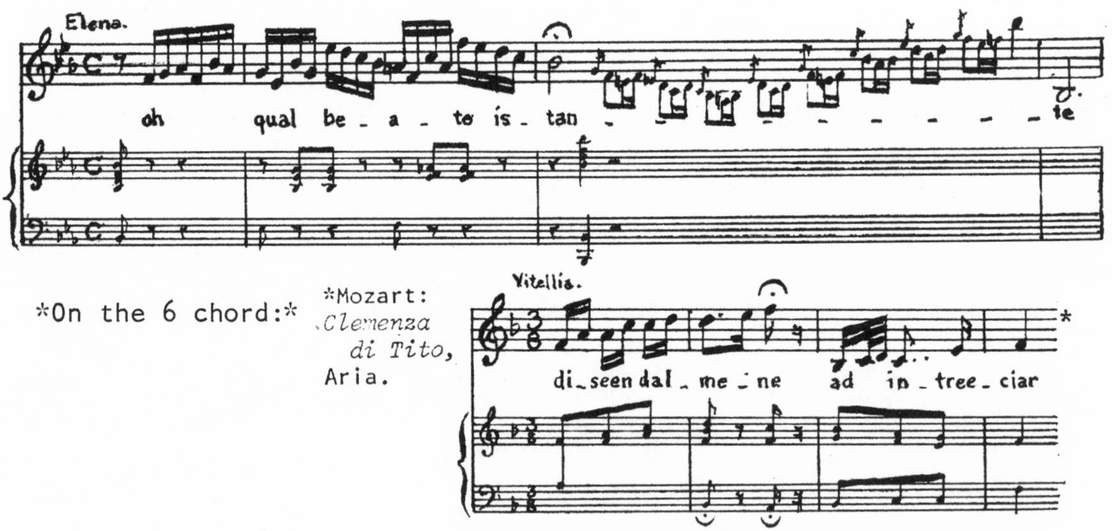

On the 6 chord: *Mozart: *Clemenza di Tito*, Aria.

On the 7 chord:

Mozart:
Clemenza di Tito.

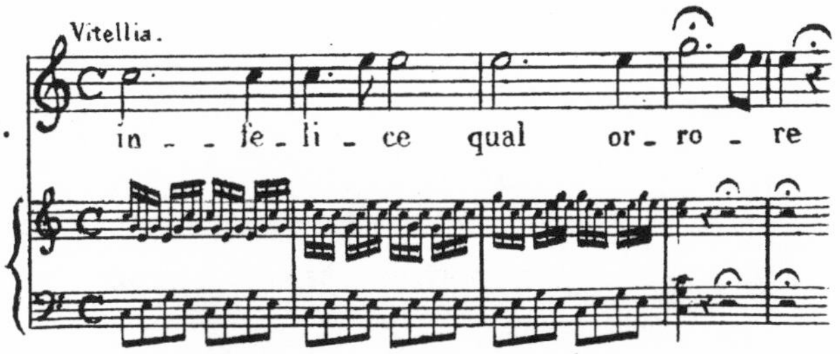

Vitellia.
in - - fe - li - ce qual or - ro - re

On the $\frac{6}{5}$ chord:

Mozart:
Nozze di Figaro,
Aria.

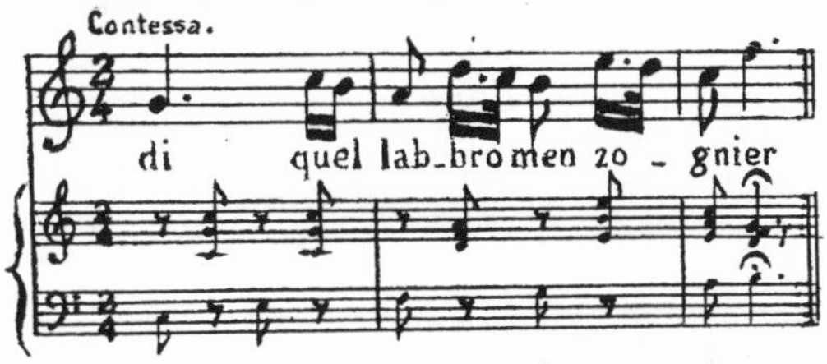

Contessa.
di quel lab_bro men zo - gnier

On the $\frac{6}{4}$ and $\frac{5}{3}$ chords:

Mozart:
Don Giovanni,
Aria.

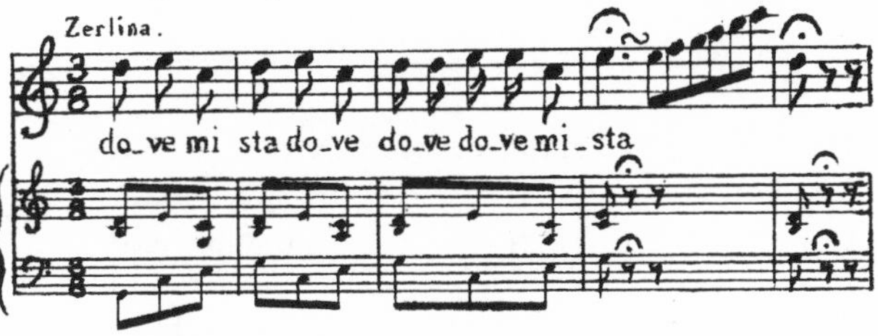

Zerlina.
do_ve mi sta do_ve do_ve do_ve mi_sta

On the $\frac{6}{4}$ and 7 chords

Rhod:
Variations.

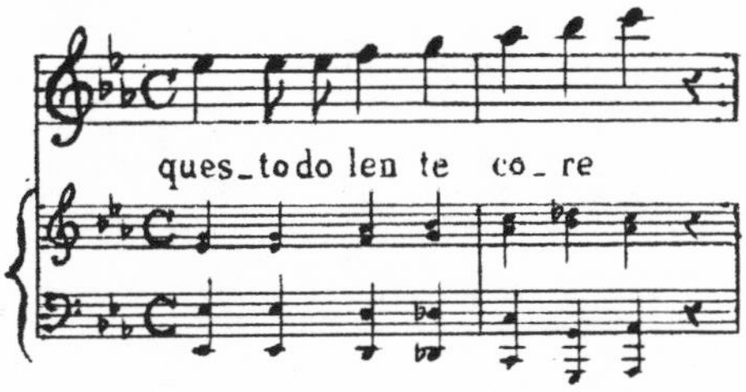

ques_to do len te co_re

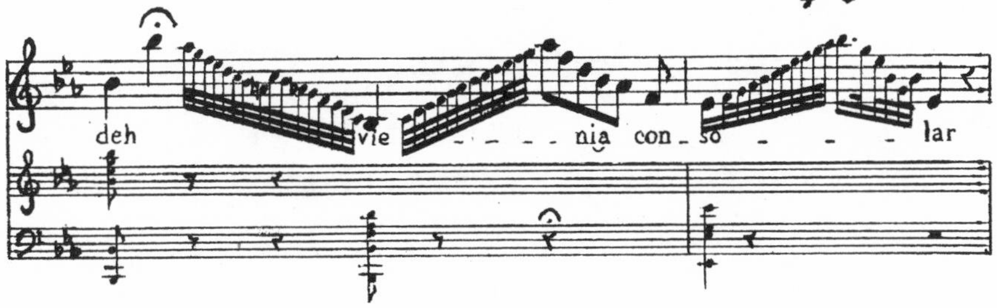

deh vie - - - - nia con_so - - - lar

On the 9 chord:

*Donizetti:
Betty,
Rondo.

Betty.
a mio ben di vo_vo ar_do - - re per te l'al ma av_vam - pe_ra

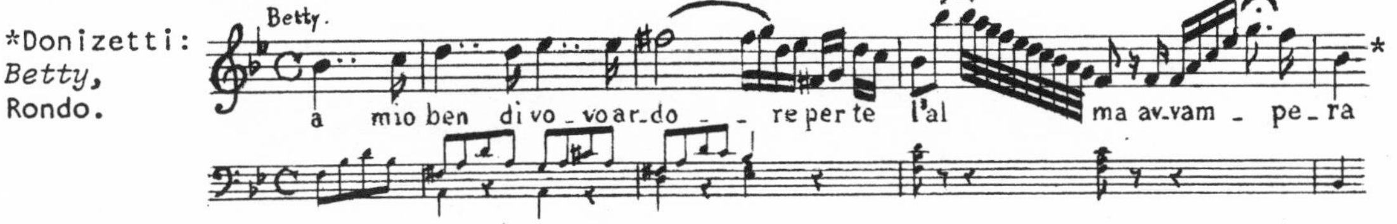

The organ points have the effect of at least doubling the length of the note or the rest which carries them, and, in nearly every kind of music, represents limits in which the singer can show his taste or display the power of his resources. During the performance of the passages, the accompaniment remains suspended. Whatever may be the imagination and facility of the student, he should be rigorously subjected to the following rules:

The organ point will be confined exclusively to the chord which carries it. Until the eighteenth century (see Baini and Reicha), the singer modulated about at the pleasure of his caprice. Today that liberty is permitted exclusively to artists who combine a profound skill [*science*] with an infallible taste.

A good example: Organ point of Madame Damoreau.

*Auber:
Le Serment,
Aria.
Marie. Andantino.
ne peu - - vent ja mais
l'ou - - - - bli - er

Although this example belongs to the celebrated singer Millico, it seems to us to be too irregular to be imitated:

Giordani:
Artaserse,
Aria.
Se al labbro mio.
Composed in 1772.
l'a man - - - - - - - - - - te cor

The organ point should be placed only on a *long syllable*. It is furthermore necessary that the singer save himself one or two syllables which will serve to end the organ point. In general, in order to end it with more energy, it is advantageous to reserve two syllables.

When the words do not offer the opportunity, one should not fear repeating the same word if the meaning permits it; in the contrary case, one should vocalize the organ point on the exclamation *ah!* Example:

The organ point should be done on a single breath. It is thus essential to measure one's capabilities and undertake only what they can accomplish. This precaution is all the more necessary when one must draw out [*filer*] the note which carries the organ point before performing the passage which follows it. One can compromise this rule, practiced in all the good schools, only by composing the organ point of several words, or by repeating the same words and by breathing in the space between them. Example:

It is better, unquestionably, to use this means than to cut the words by breathing, as several incompetent singers wrongly do it.[56]

The syllabic organ points can give, through the strength and the expression of the words, more theatrical effect to the declamatory songs. Examples: [J]

They are the resource of comic singers or of serious singers who lack agility.

---

[56]This organ point, composed principally of syllables, could be named *syllabic organ point.*

The little melodies which serve to fill the organ points and to form the *conduits* should offer a complete meaning which is in harmony with the character of the piece. It is the same with the words on which the organ points are placed.

In order to avoid monotony in expanded organ points, one composes them of two, three, and even of four different motives. *One sees some examples of them in the *conduits* of the aria from *Le Serment*.* One takes care to extablish a certain inequality between the values of the notes in the different motives or a marked variety of dynamics, two means, the use of which enlivens the little melodies and puts away the idea of a vocalise or a throat exercise. (*See the organ points at the end of the work.*)

The organ points are also placed at the beginning of some pieces with a free beginning; in the course of the melody, at certain cadences pointed out by the composer or required by the sentiment; at the end of the recitatives which are better when so ornamented. *Examples of organ point at the beginning:*

Often, in order to avoid a surplus of ornaments, one joins the two chords, the $\frac{6}{4}$ and the 7th. One thus omits the organ point which would correspond to the first chord. Example:

Bellini: *Sonnambula*, Cavatina.

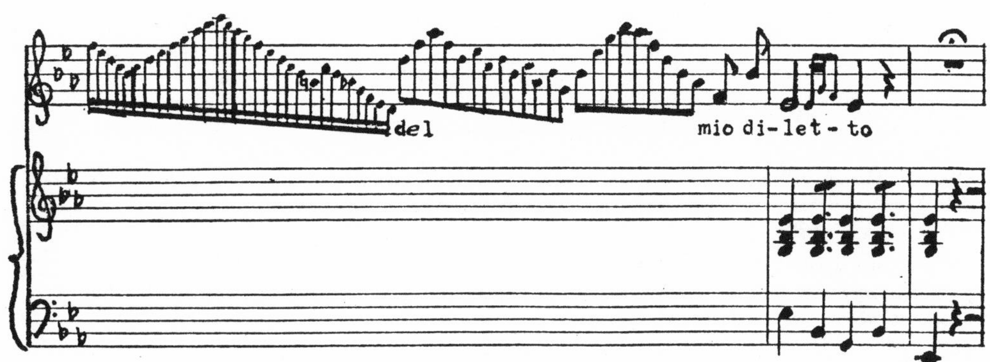
del
mio di-let-to

CHAPTER IV

EXPRESSION

The pathetic accent is the expression added to the melody. "The great law of the arts," Mr. Cousin has said, "is expression; *every work of art which does not express an idea, means nothing.*" The artist would seek vainly to have an effect on the souls of his listeners, if he did not appear himself to be vitally affected by the emotion which he would communicate to others; for it is especially through sympathy that the emotions are transmitted. One understands then that the artist produces on us only the emotions analogous to those which he feels himself; consequently there results for him the obligation to enliven, and to elevate his thoughts.

The musical performance, reduced to a simple mechanism, might it be accompanied by the most perfect correctness, if one could suppose it independent of expression, would leave the song cold and lifeless; but, it must be said, that correctness itself is only possible to the extent that it is sustained by a certain degree of warmth and energy.

It is not true that one can convey with the characteristics of truth a passion which one has never conceived. Let us say that, in order to reproduce a feeling well, it is necessary, if not to be subjected to its action, at least to present the image of it so vividly, that it may suffice to become somewhat animated in order to feel the gay or sad emotions which one is expressing. This aptitude assumes a high degree of natural sensitivity which work alone could not give, but which it increases and regularizes.

The singer, in order to familiarize himself with the accents of the emotion and prepare himself to apply them authoritatively, should perfect his own sensitivity and analyze his feelings.[57] [A]

He will begin by abandoning himself to the impressions to which each interesting subject gives rise; then he will submit them to an attentive examination, in order to learn to use them appropriately and with restraint [*avec mesure*].

1. THE EMOTIONS AND THE FEELINGS

Nature attaches to each sentiment distinctive characteristics, a timbre, an accent, a modulation of the voice, etc. If one prayed or threatened in timbres, with modulations and accents other than those required by threats or prayers, far from intimidating or touching tender feelings, one would succeed only in making himself ridiculous. Each individual has equally, in proportion to his nature and his position, a distinct way of feeling and expressing himself. The age, customs, organization and outward circumstances, etc., of each person modify the same sentiment, and require that he aptly vary the color of it. In order to discover the proper tone for each affection, and the tints [*nuances*] which it includes (the timbre, movement, the degree of force in the articulation, etc.), the student should read the words attentively, then surround himself with all the fundamental ideas which will

---

[57]It is by reflecting, much more than by practicing, that one perfects himself in the arts. (Jacquemont, II, 75.)

make the character thoroughly known to him; these precautions taken, he will recite his role by speaking it. In this last project [*travail*], he will put as much abandon and naivety as in the expression of a feeling which would be proper to it.

The true accent which is communicated to the voice when one speaks without preparation, is the base on which the singing expression is patterned. The chiaroscura, the accents, the feeling all then take an eloquent and persuasive aspect. The imitation of the natural and instinctive movements should then be, for the student, the object of a very special study; *but there is another means which will not serve less to initiate him into the secret of the emotions, and which we recommend to his zeal; here is this means; to isolate himself completely from the character which he is supposed to represent, to place himself face to face with that character in his imagination, and let him then act and sing. By reproducing faithfully the impressions which will have been suggested to him by that creation of fantasy, the artist will obtain much more striking effects than he would attain by beginning work straightway.[58] Another somewhat similar procedure would consist in

---

*[58]This advice is precisely that which Talma gave to a young man. This beginner was wearing himself out with vain efforts of declamation in the study of the role of Oreste; "You are deafening yourself: it is impossible for you to know what you are doing, because you do not know yet what you want to do; you have not determined in advance what effect you want to produce. Declaim your role without pronouncing a word. Place your character before you, and then listen to him: judge his manner of acting and his delivery; finally, when you are satisfied with the performer [*l'artiste*] which your imagination portrays for you, it is then that you can imitate him and declaim aloud." This precept of the most capable French tragic actor applies to every point in the art of

trying to remember a work of art representing a situation analogous to that of which one should treat. For example, if we had to study Desdemona's scene from the second act,

"L'error d'un infelice,"

could we not, at these words, imagine one of the numerous paintings of Mary Magdalene, her arms outstretched, imploring for her pardon at the feet of Christ? Sorrow and repentance could not take more touching forms.*

A nature scene, a beautiful engraving, a head, a pose, the sight of a landscape, the arches of a monument, etc., etc, can fortunately inspire the artist, and lend to his creation a color and a vivacity which make it approach real life. The process which we have just advised should be repeated according to each particular situation which shows the character under a new light, and to create new feelings.

I stress this last exercise, because the benefit which the mind takes from each of the completely studied details reacts powerfully on the voice, which comes to life and renders the intentions in all their fullness.

---

singing. When the singer has learned an aria, if he wishes to render it with as much expression as he can impart to it and to embellish it with all the ornaments which the melody and the nature of the piece permit, he must concern himself with the conception before thinking of the performance. He must sing mentally, as it were, while his imagination places before him the character he will portray. When he has thus strongly conceived the dramatic situation, when he is well penetrated by the emotion traced by the composer, in short, when he has created for himself an ideal which is as perfect as possible, it is only then that he will put to work all his imitative faculties, that he will display all his means of expression and execution, in order to approach the pattern which his thought has offered to him as a model.*

*Sometimes, while giving advice to bring out each feeling, we do not want to say that it is necessary to create [*rendre*] the image of each word and express it separately. One would succeed only in being wrong and childish at the same time. One will apply himself to each of the details only in proportion to its importance with regard to the total work.*

*This first exercise has the aim of warming the soul and making the most sympathetic accents spring forth from it, those which only a vigorous instinct can inspire. But in order that these effects be not only the result of the capricious inspirations of instinct, it is necessary, when they appear, to subject them to analysis like all the other facets [*parties*] of the art.*

The singer, even when he feels the most vivid transports of emotion, should retain enough freedom of mind to analyze the signs by means of which these transports are manifested, in order to judge them one by one, and to submit them to a scrupulous examination.[59] This important operation will give the secret of the material processes, the principal ones of which are going to be the object of our attention.

2. THE ANALYSIS

Up to now we have excluded, like so many grave errors, the use of the dampened [*étouffés*] and shrill [*criards*] timbres, the trembling of

---

[59]A skillful and sustained practice permits us to succeed in expressing the most vivid emotion while remaining completely cold ourselves. Talma, in the last years of his career, carried this art to its final limits.

the tone, the noisy breath, or one placed in the middle of a word, etc., etc. We had to state the general principles which answered the first need of the art; we considered the voice as an instrument whose range, purity and flexibility, elements necessary for correctness of style, had to be developed. Now our task increases; we are arriving at the most intimate resources of the skill [*science*], at the irregular means which appear defective, which it is permissible, even advisable, to use under the inspiration of a bold and impassioned movement.

The signs by which man indicates emotion are:

1. Facial movements.
2. The various alterations of the breathing.
3. The excitement [*émotion*] of the voice.
4. The different timbres.
5. The alteration of the articulation.
6. The movement of the delivery [*débit*].
7. The elevation or lowering of the tones.
8. The various degrees of intensity of the voice.

Each of these subjects is going to give rise to some new observations.

Facial Expression (*Physionomie*).[60]

Everything abides in man, and each movement of the soul is made

---

[60]Garrick would instantly change expression and assume the most opposite physiognomies in the shortest time which sufficed to hide himself behind a door and to reappear immediately. (See Grimm, IV, 350-370.)

felt in the entire harmonious arrangement; it results that the movement and the voice should be naturally in accord in the expression of the same thought; for example, anger is betrayed by the outward action and by the excitement of the voice at the same time. It is the same with the other emotions.[61] The facial expression of the character traits fortifies the vocal expression, which it serves to make more striking and more persuasive. This harmony of the character and the voice is the usual procedure, that of every frank emotion. The discord between the outward action and the accent of the voice can only be the expression of a vivid emotion which one seeks to conceal: it is thus that embarassment, lying, etc., are betrayed. Thus then, to impart to the face and the voice two different expressions would be a true misrepresentation.

Alterations in the Breathing.

The breathing undergoes, in proportion to the state of the soul, very diverse modifications: it is sometimes steady [*posée*] and long, sometimes short and agitated, noisy, jerky, gasping, etc.; sometimes it is transformed into bursts of laughter, into sobs, into sighs, etc. We are going to concern ourselves only with the most difficult procedures to perform, namely: the sighs, sobs, and laughter.

---

[61]This fundamental idea makes understood the necessity of two distinct studies which have as objectives, one the voice, the other pantomime. The facial expression shows principally in the eyes and the mouth; the exalted passions shine, so to speak, from these two points, they extend and reach the face, the head, the limbs and set the entire body into motion.

Sighs and Sobs

Sighs, in all their varieties, are produced by the stronger or weaker, longer or shorter rubbing of the air against the walls of the throat, either when one takes the air into the chest, or when one lets it out. When one uses the first method one can modify the friction in such a way as to obtain the sob, even the rattle [*râle*], if the vocal cords are activated. Sobs are obtained by a short and jerky inhalation. Examples of sobs:

Mozart: *Don Giovanni*, Aria.

The rattle is an accent which is never turned into a musical sound.

When one has recourse to the second means, that is to say, to the expulsion of the air, one produces the sigh properly so-called and the groan. The sigh precedes a note or follows it. When the sigh precedes the note, if it is placed on a vowel, it converts it into a sung exhalation; if it is placed on a consonant, it forms, before that consonant, the sound *heu!* [hø] aspirated. Example:

Rossini: *Otello*, First Finale.

Desdemona.
L'er_ror l'error d'un in _ fe _ li _ ce ha padre
heu! l'error heu! l'error d'un in _ fe_

When the sigh ends the note, it is produced by a strong expulsion of air. Example:

p

a ah! pa_dre a ah! pa dreh!

Or else one first lets the voice fall in order to then push out the air, which produces a moan [*plainte*]. Example:

Mozart: *Don Giovanni*, Recitative.

Dª Anna.
pa_dre mi_o ca_ro pa_dre ah pa_drea_ma_to
a ah! pa

The sigh is also obtained by means of an ascending portamento which one muffles by the noise of the air. This portamento, at its beginning, should be only the friction of the air. Example:

ha h!

Let us add finally that the exhalation also produces a kind of friction or tearing of the voice; but, although the effect of it is dramatic, the study of it is too laborious for us to dare to advise it.

All these procedures formed by the inhalation and the exhalation are combined in different ways, as one sees in the following examples.

Rossini: *Otello*, Romance.

Desdemona.
ma stanh calh fin heudi sparge_re mes_ti sos_pi _ rie pian _ to heumo.

*Donizetti: *Lucie*, Translated aria.

Laughter

Laughter is a kind of convulsive spasm which permits the voice to escape only by jerks and shakes. It traverses then, in ascending and in descending, a somewhat irregular scale, but a rather lengthy one. The breath requires frequent and rapid renewal, and this need, added to the contraction which takes place in the vocal organ, brings about at each inhalation a rather loud rattle. In the pieces one should avoid as much as possible the stiffness and coldness of the written note; one should, on the contrary, imitate the abandon and the cantilena of the natural laugh. A free and musically rhythmic laugh can be obtained only as a result of long practice. *Examples:*

Laughter belongs exclusively to comic opera; serious opera can permit it only in a painful feeling disguised by a forced laughter, or in a case of insanity [*la folie*].

The Emotion of the Voice

There is a kind of inner agitation which comes to us from the fullness of an experienced feeling, and which is betrayed outwardly by the faltering *or the hysteria [*nerf*]* of the voice, and from the delivery. This state of the soul, which is called emotion, is the necessary disposition which should take place with anyone who wants to act powerfully on others. If this agitation is caused by indignation, excessive joy, terror, exaltation, etc., the voice is emitted by a kind of shake. Examples:

Agitation caused by fear:

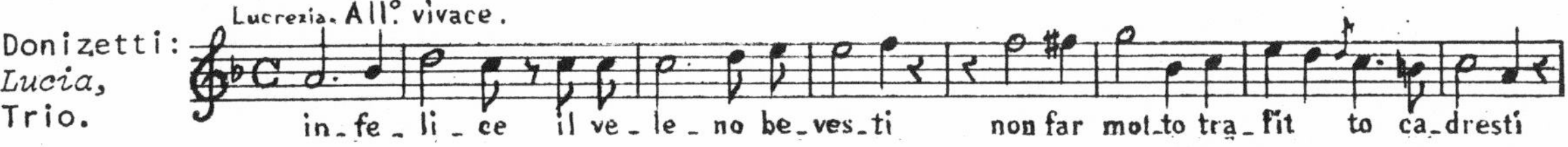

Agitation caused by joy:

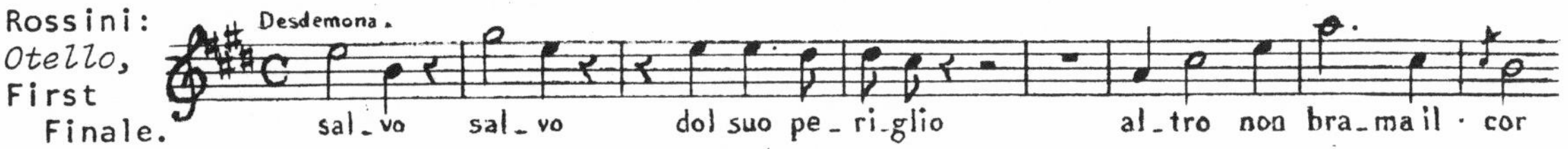

Agitation caused by indignation:

Agitation caused by indignation and anger:

Agitation caused by fear and remorse:

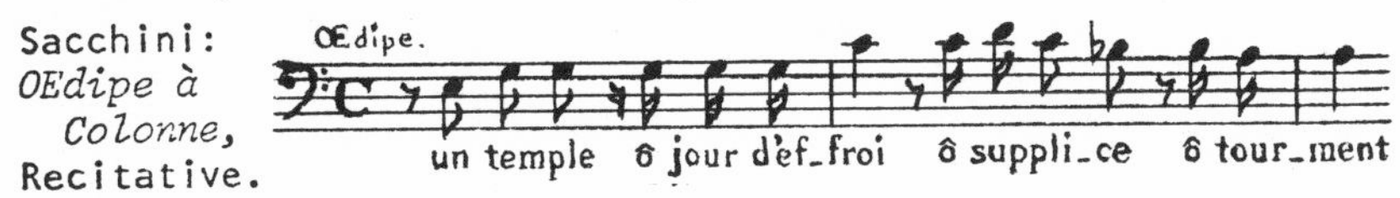

Agitation caused by indignation, contempt and despair:

When the same agitation is produced by a grief so vivid that it completely dominates us, the organ experiences a kind of vacillation which is imparted to the voice. This vacillation is called *tremolo*. The tremolo, motivated by the situation and managed with art, has a certain moving effect [*un effet pathétique assuré*]. Examples:

Do not sing, but declaim, with a heart-rending and most disordered voice, the words: "*Raoul! they will kill you*," then with the respiration oppressed and becoming feeble, finish the words: "*Ah! pity! I am dying! ah!*"

The tremolo should be used only to portray the feelings which, in real life, move us profoundly: the anguish of seeing someone who is dear to us in imminent danger, the tears which certain movements of anger or of vengeance draw from us, etc. Even in these circumstances, the use of it should be regulated with taste and moderation [*mesure*]; as soon as one exaggerates the expression or the length of it, it becomes tiresome and awkward. Outside of the special cases which we have just indicated, it is necessary to guard against altering in any way the security of the sound, for the repeated use of the tremolo makes the voice tremulous [*chevrotante*]. The artist who has contracted this intolerable fault becomes incapable of phrasing any kind of sustained song. It is thus that some beautiful voices have been lost to the art.

The quavering of the voice is, in all the possible cases, only an affectation of feeling which certain people take for a true feeling. Some singers believe, wrongly, that their voices are made more vibrant by this means, and, the same as several violinists, seek to increase the strength of their instruments by the undulation of the sound. The voice can vibrate only thanks to the brilliance of the timbre and the power of the emission of the air, and not by the effect of the tremor.

The Timbres (*Metalli della voce*).

A few tries suffice to ascertain that each emotion, however slight the shade of it may be, will appropriately affect the vocal organ by modifying the capacity, the conformation, the rigidity, in short, all the physical conditions of it. The organ is therefore a mould which is constantly transformed under the action of the various emotions, and imparts their imprint to the sounds which it emits. Thanks to its admirable flexibility, this organ also aids, up to a certain point, in the description of exterior objects, as one can observe even in simple conversation. If it concerns, for example, representing a hollow, long [*étendu*] or thin object, the voice produces, by a mimicking movement, hollow, long or thin, etc., sounds.

The timbres are such an essential part of the discourse, they are so truly the condition of a sincere feeling, that one could not be negligent in the choice of it without falling infallibly into error. There are those which reveal the intimate feeling which the words do not always express sufficiently, and which they sometimes even tend to contradict. *The pieces which portray indecision, troubled thought, irony, poorly restrained grief, require only the mixture and instability of the timbres; also it is necessary to express each of these feelings by the kind of disorder which is appropriate to it; wherever the idea is precise, the timbre maintains its unity.*

*We have said above (see Part One, chapter III); that the sombre timbre (*metallo oscuro*, or *coperto*) was produced when the tube was deep and bent at a right angle by the lowering of the larynx; while on the contrary, the clear timbre (*metallo chiaro*, or *aperto*) is obtained when the buccal tube is slightly curved, the larynx is presented at the isthmus of the throat. At the point at which we have arrived, these notions do not suffice at all. It is necessary to know that the lips of the glottis can vibrate equally, either when the posterior extremities are put into contact (by the bringing together of the internal processes of the arytenoids), or when these extremities remain separated. In the first case, the sounds are emitted with all the brilliance possible; in the second, the voice takes a dull character.[62]*

---

*[62]This important idea merits some developments. When one very vigorously pinches the arytenoids together, the glottis is represented only by a narrow or elliptical slit, through which the air driven out by the lungs must escape. Here each molecule of air is subjected to the laws of vibrations, and the voice takes on a very pronounced brilliance. If, on the contrary, the arytenoids are separated, the glottis assumes the shape of an isoceles triangle, the little side of which is formed between the arytenoids. One can then produce only extremely dull notes, and, in spite of the weakness of the resulting sounds, the air escapes in such abundance that the lungs are exhausted in a few moments. This enormous expenditure of air, which coincides with the production of

This brilliance or this dull color of the tones can indistinctly modify the clear timbre and the sombre timbre, and offer the student a throng of resources which permit him to appropriately vary the expression of the voice.[63] [B]

The examples which follow will serve to illustrate the importance of this observation. The curse of Edgardo:

---

veiled tones, indicates, according to us, that the glottis assumes the triangular form. One understands in fact that the air does not encounter any resistance toward the base of the triangle, and that it passes freely through the glottis almost without receiving any vibrations from it. It is only at the summit of the angle which parts from the thyroid cartilage that the condensations and rarefactions of the air are formed in a complete manner. Likewise, but in the opposite way, the brilliance of the sounds and the fourfold or fivefold duration of the breath indicate that the organ is offering no more than a linear or elliptical slit. Let us add that when we pinch the glottis strongly, we synergistically bring about a certain contraction, a kind of condensation of the tissues of the pharynx, most favorable states for the vitality [*nerf*] and the brilliance of the voice. On the contrary, the separation of the arytenoids brings about the softness of these same tissues, as a result of which, the sonorous waves, absorbed or poorly reflected, lose nearly all their brilliance. One sees, according to what precedes, that the timbre depends not only upon the modifications which the tube imparts to the sonorous waves, but also upon the place where these vibrations are born; that is to say that the voice receives its first character in the glottis, then from the numerous modifications of the pharyngeal and buccal cavities. One can summarize what precedes in this principle: *that each modification in the mode of production of the vibrations develops a different timbre, and each modification which the tube through which it passes undergoes modifies the original timbre.**

[63]We are recalling here a rule stated above (see pages 7-8), and which is this: the modifications of timbre which the tones undergo depend upon the position which they occupy in the range. The range included between the notes $e\flat^1$ and c^2 in the chest with tenors will correspond to the open timbre of the lower tones, not with absolutely the same timbre, but with a clearer shade of the same timbre. [C] This observation is also applied to the head voice compared to the falsetto voice in women. The chest register should likewise receive on the notes $e\flat^1$ to $f\#^1$ a more rounded shade than the lower notes.

Maledetto sia l'istante
(Donizetti: *Lucia*, Finale.)

requires not only the clear timbre, but also all the brilliance of the voice. On the contrary, the words:

Io credeva che alcuno
(Rossini: *Otello*, Recitative.)

should, because of the mental exhaustion which is overwhelming Desdemona, be pronounced with a clear, but smothered and colorless voice. The arrogant challenge of Otello:

Or or vedrai qual chiudo
(Rossini: *Otello*, Duet.)

can be rendered only in a round and bursting voice; while the terror which takes possession of Assur at the sight of the shadow of Ninus:

Deh! ti ferma, ti placa, perdona
(Rossini: *Semiramide*, Aria.)

requires, in order to be truthful, the use of the sombre timbre and the muffled voice. If we should try to change in these examples the characters of the voice, the clear, the sombre, the brilliant and the dull, the effect of it would be detestable. This use made of the mistaken interpretation explains why the sounds which please in certain movements, displease elsewhere; why the unvarying singer recites only certain passages well. The clear and brilliant timbre, used out of its place, seems shrill; the clear and dull timbre, inane; the sombre and brilliant timbre seems grumbling; the sombre and dull timbre produces the effect of hoarseness.

The choice of the timbre will never depend on the literal meaning of the words, but on the movements of the soul which dictates them. The tender and languorous feelings, or even also the energetic, but concentrated feelings, do not go beyond the series of sombre timbres. For example: in prayer, timidity, pity, the voice should be moving and slightly covered. Sometimes the noise of the breath is mixed with it in the feeling of tenderness. Examples:

Indignation, cursing, threatening and severe commands round the voice and make it abrupt, haughty. Examples:

Warlike or religious exhaltation round the voice while making it clear and brilliant. Examples:

Religious exhaltation:

Restrained threat, profound grief and repressed [*concentré*] despair take a hollow [*caverneux*] timbre. Examples:

Threat stirred up by profound hate:

Here the accents of grief are shaded, sometimes by a tint of melancholy, sometimes by bursts of sorrow, sometimes by a dark despair.

Terror and mystery muffle the tones, and make them sombre and raucous. Examples:

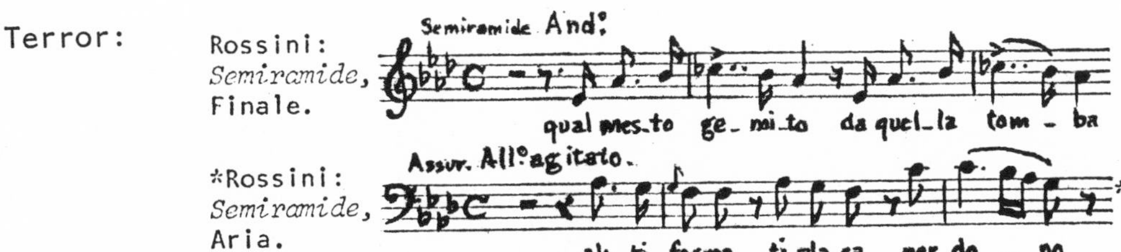

*Meyerbeer: *Robert le diable*: Duet.

Mystery and threat:

Mystery shaded by terror and indignation:

In the depression which follows a strong disturbance, the voice is emitted dully, because the breath cannot be held back, and is mixed into the tones. Examples:

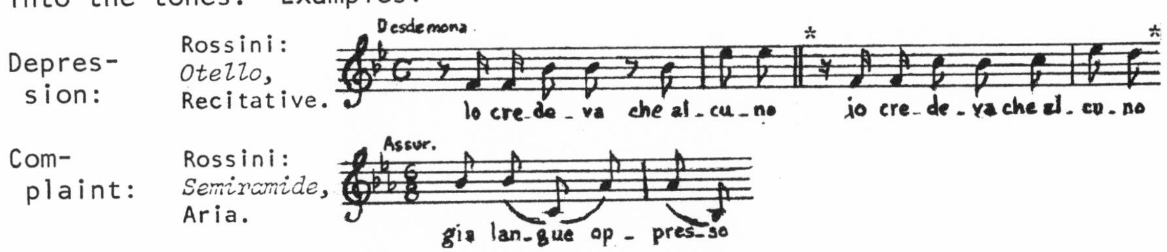

This dull character of the voice is the opposite of the brilliant, metallic timbre, which corresponds to vigorous feelings.

This first series of timbres forms a contrast with that which cheerful feelings produce, or also the frightful feelings, but which are given up without coercion.

The gentle and affectionate character which the vocal organ takes to express love partakes more of the clear timbre than of the sombre timbre. Examples:

In joy, the timbre becomes vivid, brilliant and supple [*délié*].

Examples:

Frank gaiety:

Mozart: *Don Giovanni*, Aria.

In laughter, the voice is shrill and yelping, interrupted, convulsive. Example:

Laughter:

Teasing makes the organ metallic, shrill. Example:

Teasing:

Meyerbeer: *Robert le diable*, Duet.

Threat, grief and despair which burst adopt the open and rending timbre. One sees some remarkable examples of it in the passages which follow:

Threat and bursting anger:

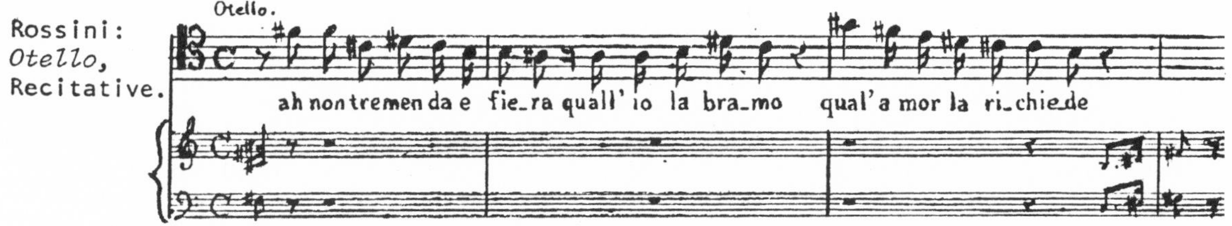

Heart-rending grief:

The chest tones above f^1 are intolerable when one uses them in restrained songs; but here, for the very reason of their shrill effect, they adapt themselves to the accents of despair and rage. One could say much about it in the passage:

From the observations which precede there follow, it seems to us, several important consequences:

1. The tones lacking brilliance, used in a *just* measure and in a suitable timbre, should serve to express the feelings which disturb the soul and bring about the collapse of the vocal organs. These feelings are tenderness, timidity, fear, embarrassment, terror, etc. On the contrary, the sounds which have all their brilliance serve to express the feelings which excite the energy of the organs, vivid joy, anger, rage, arrogance, etc.

2. The two series of opposed timbres follow a course parallel to that of the emotions. The timbres set out from an intermediary point, where the expression of gentle feelings is placed, then they separate in opposite directions. The timbres arrive at their last exaggeration when the emotions themselves have attained their final limit; the lively emotions or the frightful ones which burst with violence take the open timbres. The serious feelings, openly voiced [*élevés*] or repressed [*concentrés*], take the covered timbres.[64]

These first two series of facts, produced by the alteration of the breathing and by the use of the different timbres, form an inarticulate language, composed of tears, interjections, cries, sighs, etc.,

---

[64]The character of these timbres is necessarily related to the age and to the nature of the organ of each individual; let us even say that in young singers extreme freshness should be the dominant quality: it indicates an organ which is in all its virginity. When a voice has been experienced by the emotions, age and work, it is modified; the freshness and the brilliance of the timbre make way for solidity and volume. Some young people make the error of wanting to imitate the organs of artists matured by the stage and by years, and by means of obstinacy, they succeed in aging their voices before their time. Sometimes, by a contrary error, some singers, already aged, borrow, in order to rejuvenate themselves, a childish timbre. The voice, like everything else, should follow the progress of time.

which one could properly name the language of the soul. These means can affect still more powerfully than the word, and take birth principally in the lungs and the pharynx. The exact knowledge of this last part of the vocal instrument in its relation to these kinds of products should be familiar to every dramatic singer, and will become the principal source of his success.[65]

---

*[65]We will terminate this chapter on the timbres by some important observations on the kind of voice incorrectly named the mixed voice, or *mezzo petto*; their rather technical nature advises us to put them into the form of a footnote.*

In France, the highest part of the chest voice, including from f^1 to c^2, is given the name of mixed voice [*voix mixte*], whether the voice presents in this range the characters of the sombre timbre, or, on the contrary, the tones are excessively clear and sharp [*deliées*]. In Italy this same range is called, in the first case, *voce di petto*, and in the second, *voce di mezzo petto*. Whatever the character of these tones may be, they belong to the chest register, but with a modification of volume with which we are going to concern ourselves. The designations of *voix mixte* and *mezzo petto* are equally improper, for they would make us suppose that these clear and high pitched tones are produced by the two mechanisms of the chest and falsetto registers at the same time. Now, physiologically, the simultaneous conjunction of two different mechanisms serving to produce the same note, or two notes in unison, is an unacceptable idea. In fact, the production of any one sound places the organ into entirely different and irreconcilable conditions, according as it is formed by the mechanism of the chest voice or that of the falsetto. The conformity of position could be encountered only in the simultaneous emission of two notes of different pitch. But then one would have to ask oneself if it is possible for the larynx to simultaneously produce two distinct tones. This possibility would be admissible by supposing a larynx shaped in such a manner that the different registers remain independent of each other in their mechanism. The history of music furnishes several examples of this phenomenon (see Part One). The thin character of the high tones of the so-called [*prétendue*] mixed voice results only, according to us, *from the vibrations of the vocal cords*, without the cooperation of the pharynx to reinforce them. One knows in fact that the intensity of a tone depends in general upon the number of partials which vibrate concurrently to form it, and upon the amplitude [*étendue*] of the vibrations which these partials execute; as a consequence, by reducing the number of vibrating partials, one decreases the sound. Moreover, it is demonstrated that the glottis, by the gradual tension of its lips and the successive reduction of its dimensions, produces the entire series of chest tones; but the vibrations generated in the glottis acquire all their power only provided that they are extended into the ventricles, then into the pharynx. According to that, one understands that if it were possible to limit the vibrations to the glottis by reducing the ventricles and the pharynx to a purely passive role, one would have the thinnest tones possible. It is in fact this result that a capable singer knows how to obtain, when on one side he completely relaxes all the muscles of the pharynx, and on the other he narrows more and more the column of air. In these circumstances, the glottis, endowed with a complete liberty, can reach the final limits of its action. One is astonished to see tenors give, without any apparent effort, the notes a^1, b^1, c^2, $c\#^2$, d^2. For women, and especially for children, in whom the glottis is very narrow at the same time as the arytenoideous muscles are very delicate, one does not know how high that series of tones might rise: we presume, *a priori*, that it would go at least to the g^2. We always advise that it is well if these notes are replaced in practice by the falsetto tones, preferable in all respects. If, while the glottis alone vibrates and all other parts of the instrument are relaxed, one moderately increases the pressure of the air, one obtains an increase of brilliance and intensity, but never an increase of volume. One can conceive the immense advantage which the male voice can draw from these observations, completely new in theory, and too rarely applied instinctively by some artists. They serve to clarify the relatively high notes ordinarily so thick in basses, baritones, and tenors. They indicate to these latter the mechanism to practice [*suivre*] to increase the range of the chest register; they permit the *piano* and *mezza voce* use of this register in the high tones and thus the dispensation of the excessive use of the falsetto tones; finally, they facilitate the union of the registers, etc.*

The list of facts which we have just enumerated is completely modified when the contraction of the pharyngeal muscles is added to that of the glottis.

*The instrument then forms a single whole which the excessively held column can no longer make vibrate, but which was sufficient to set the glottis alone into motion. A vigorous thrust here becomes indispensable to put the entire mass into action. The voice in this case has all its amplitude and power, but can no longer reach the extraordinary notes which concern us. The $b\flat^1$, b^1, and the c^2 require energetic efforts which in the preceding hypothesis would not be appropriate. The glottis is pinched as much as the tone which one wants to produce requires, but the column of air, too powerful for its muscular strength, obliges it to enlarge and to lower the pitch. I am fully aware of it, a very strong thrust raises the pitch without the need of new contractions; but this procedure does not entirely remedy the weakness of the vocal cords. The reduction of size is already a fact in the clear timbre, where no infrahyoideous muscles come into action to counteract the action of the arytenoideous muscles; but it is especially striking, if we produce the sounds in the sombre timbre [*voix sombrée, voix mixte*];

Alterations of the Articulation.

The articulation, by its various degrees of energy and its alterations, marks the shades of the different emotions, and strengthens the expression of the feelings. It is energetic in the vigorous and animated movements. That is what takes place in the words of the following passages:

C'était aux palmes du martyre à couronner tant de vertus
(Rossini: *Guillaume Tell*, Final cadences of the Trio.)

Trema, trema, scellerato,
(Mozart: *Don Giovanni*, First finale.)

Fuggi, crudele, fuggi
(Mozart: *Don Giovanni*, Duet.)

Ah! vieni, nel tuo sangue
(Rossini: *Otello*, Duet.)

Parti, crudel, etc.
(Rossini: *Otello*, First finale.)

oh! cielo rendimi
(Rossini: *Gazza ladra*, Duet.)

Coppia iniqua
(Donizetti: *Anna Bolena*, Rondo.)

Largo al factotum
(Rossini: *Barbiere di Siviglia*, Aria.)

Fin ch'han dal vino
(Mozart: *Don Giovanni*, Aria.)

---

the lips of the glottis must then, by their own contractive force, resist not only the column of air, but also the opposed and considerable force of the depressor muscles, which tend to open the thyroid cartilage and to separate these same lips. Some extraordinary efforts can momentarily overcome this resistance; but exhaustion and paralysis of the organ are the inevitable and unfortunately too frequent result of the use of this procedure.*

Amor, perchè mi pizzichi
(Fioraventi: Aria.)

Un segreto d'importanza
(Cimarosa: *Matrimonio segreto*, Duet.)

Un bel uso
(Rossini: *Turco in Italia*, Duet.)

The articulation softens in tender and gracious movements. The following pieces can serve as examples:

Voi che sapete
(Mozart: *Nozze di Figaro*, Aria.)

Batti, batti,
(Mozart: *Don Giovanni*, Aria.)

Deh! calma, ciel,
(Rossini: *Otello*.)

Descends,
(Auber: *La Muette*.)

Trouble, shame, terror, etc., are prejudicial to the firmness of the organs: the voice becomes stammering. Sobs, choking and anguish end up by making it irregular. Examples:

Whatever accidents that the syllabication may experience, the singer will never forget that the listener must understand the words with perfect clarity; for if there is even a moment of indistinctness, the action loses all its interest. The need for clarity is especially obvious in the whispering of the pianissimo, where nothing could replace it.

The Movement of the Delivery (See Recitative).

The Raising or Lowering of the Tones (See *Alterations*, chapter III).

The Intensity of the Voice.

The choice of the part of the voice which corresponds best to a feeling belongs to the composer. However, the singer, in order to place the alterations which his organ requires, or the ornaments which the feeling suggests to him, can depart from this principle, so that in white voices, the medium and low parts are more moving than the high, and that this latter, on the contrary, corresponds better to brilliant effects. In men, the high tones of the chest register are the ones which contain the characteristics of expression.

Regarding the different degrees of intensity, see the article on *Inflection and Dynamics*.

3. UNITY

The art uses all the procedures of performance; but it does not use them all indifferently and by chance. On the contrary, it calls to its aid only the resources which suit the particular need of each situation, of each movement. This strict and intelligent choice of means and effects constitutes what one calls *unity*.[66] One can define it: the perfect agreement among the diverse parts of a whole. The skill [*science*] which makes all the efforts of the talent converge toward a single end, and multiplies the power of the means because of their harmony, is the last degree of perfection in all the arts. Now, this difficult science rests on the exact intelligence of the value of the ideas.

In order to obey this principle of unity, in particular applications, the singer should first make himself a fixed idea of the primary emotion which governs in the piece. Usually, each emotion fills by its developments one of the large divisions of a musical piece, designated by the words *adagio*, *andante*, *allegro*, etc. In the pieces composed of several divisions, one reserves for the slow movements the expression of terror, surprise, abatement [of a conflict] and restrained feelings. The lively feelings, such as furor, threat, outbursts of joy, enthusiasm, war-like ardor, etc., are included in the animated rhythms. After having studied the dominant emotion of the piece, one will pass to the examination of the particular feelings which develop it or modify it. One will determine which purposes should be highlighted, and which

---

*[66]One sins against unity when one makes use of resources which are good in themselves, but which are not appropriate to the need of the movement which is being expressed. Let us say even: in such a case, the more powerful and brilliant the means being used is, the more one is shocked by the error committed. In a theater in Genoa, a singer was displaying a powerful and sonorous voice in the phrase:

"Mi manca la voce, mi sento morire" (Rossini: *Mose*, Quartet.)
when suddenly a listener called to him from the orchestra:

Ti cresce, non ti manca la voce, sor asino!
Everything must be judged, not at all in isolation by itself, but in its relationship to the general effect.*

others should be relegated to a secondary level; which effects should be led into gradually [*par gradation*], which others produced by contrast.

The unity of the dominant emotion is found and made felt in the most unexpected contrasts, as well as in the best controlled transitions. Thus we see Otello fall prey by turns to love, to rage, to fierce joy, to tears, and yet we accept this aggregate; we understand the unity of all these opposed movements, because such are the outbursts, such is the normal progress of jealosy. That emotion is here the center to which all these different emotions lead, and where they are tied together.

On that important question of transitions and contrasts, it is difficult or impossible to state precise rules. The success of the transitions depends less on the number and the length of the details which compose them than it does upon the fortunate choice of these details and on the skilled use which one knows how to make of them. The correctness of the conceptions of the artist and the feeling [*tact*] with which he presents them makes the listener enter immediately into the same impression. It is the privilege of the great artist to take hold of our mind and our soul at one stroke. Meanwhile one can say in general that the emotion can neither heat up nor be extinguished instantaneously, and it is necessary, when contrasts follow one another all at once, to hold up to view only those feelings with an equal intensity [*vivacité*]. The soul, once set into motion, can pass over all distances, but cannot stop abruptly.

The artist, in order to impart to the public the general

impression which he has put into a piece, must apply himself to the principal means which determine the character of the performance, to the movement, to the expression of the voice, etc.

It is a question here of grasping well what distinguishes one *cantabile* from another *cantabile*, one *agitato* from another *agitato*; for example, the cantabile *Casta diva* is stamped with an extasy full of tenderness and dignity, while the cantabile *Fra poco a me ricovero* paints the despondency of a soul broken by grief. As to the particular ideas, one studies the intention and performance of them in each period, in each phrase, taken one after the other. One must choose, among the shades of feeling which express these ideas, the tint which is the most appropriate to the dominant emotion.

One will choose in particular the chiaroscuro, the accentuation, the degree of ornamentation, the timbre, etc., which makes them worth more in themselves and in their relationship to what precedes and what follows. The phrase: *Frères ingrats, je devrais vous haïr* (aria from *Joseph*), seems to express threat, and yet the grief which Joseph feels requires that it be said with emotion, and not with harshness.

The same accents are not always suitable in situations which at first approach appear identical. Thus Desdemona and Norma, both guilty women, beg their father's pardon for a transgression; but the one prays for herself, and scarcely dares it, held back by confusion and shame; the other, on the contrary, forgets her humiliation, and prays with the anguish, the vehemence of a mother who fears for her child. The slightest modification in the feelings influences the expression and suffices to change the character of it.

Tears, fury and fierce joy are common to Shylock and Othello; but the one, vilified and persecuted usurer, nourishes a muffled hatred against his oppressors; the other a generous and fierce warrior, abandons himself with rage to outbursts of jealousy.

Finally the student should not neglect any traits of character, not even the minutest. No detail is so unimportant that it does not have a place in the total. "Anything is much" [*rien, c'est beaucoup*], said Voltaire.

The member of the phrase, the motives, the quantity, the important word, the progressions, the partial inflections, the appoggiaturas, the drawn out [*filés*] sounds, the portamentos, the stolen [*dérobés*] beats, demand all our attention. It is necessary to ask oneself which of the accent or the ornaments depicts an image best, which of these two means most suitably varies the return of the same ideas, etc. From this examination, in which one applies himself to discovering everything that suits one piece more than any other, in which one shapes all the traits of character to the profit of the dominant idea, will come forth the variety, the harmony and the originality of the delivery.

What we have just said about a piece applies equally to an entire role. It is necessary to envision that role in its general character, then think of adapting the details of it to the character being represented rather than to any other. To attribute to each character, each personality what is individually his own is the way for the singer to convert all his roles into as many personalities striking with vigor and originality.

The aggregation of the things which we have just examined is found in a more or less developed manner in every phrase; the fragment of recitative: [D]

oh Di_o qual mai stre_pito e ques_to qual pre_sa gio fu_nes_to

is divided into two effects. *The first depicts an involuntary movement of fright: it is a cry of distress, a vivid emotion which must be rendered by means of bursting and firm tones, and with a marked vigor in the articulation of the syllables *Di*, *stre* and *ques*.*

*The second line depicts a reflection on himself, an inner terror. The hollow timbre, the force of the syllabication and the slowness of the delivery are the means which are suitable here. Moreover, the syllables *sa* and *nes* will be long. One will make use of the mordant to impart to the first an expression of vigor.*

The following fragment:

Rossini: *Otello*, Romanza Recitative.

lo crede_va che al_cuno oh! co_me il cielo s'uni_sce a miei la _ mento
Languid voice.
equal values.
f Poignant grief.
f
Sob.
Long and tremulous.
Groaning.
Io crede_va che al_cuno oh! co _ me il cie _ lo s'uni_sce a mie ih! hla_mento

gives rise to analogous observations. By the words:

Io credeva che alcuno,

Desdemona expresses the abatement which follows a violent commotion. In the following lines:

Ah! come il Cielo s'unisce ai miei lamenti!

grief recaptures all its empire. Monotonous and almost toneless sounds, due to faulty breathing, are sufficient to make the first effect. The second requires more complicated and incomparably more energetic means. It is necessary that the exclamation *Ah!* be emitted with violence and as though through sobs; that the syllables *co* and *cie* be struck and sustained with force; that the syllable *miei* receive a *mordent* in addition to the *prolongation* and the *appoggiatura*; finally, that the words *miei* ...*lamenti* be full of emotion and separated by a groan.

If we change style [*genre*], the effects will be different, but also quite complex. Take the cavatina:

Rossini: *Il Barbiere di Siviglia*, Cavatina.

Count.
ec-co ri-den-te il cie - - lo spun-ta la bel-la au - ro - - ra

The first member of the phrase is subjected to the crescendo. In addition, it is indispensable to bring out [*faire ressortir*] the inflections of the notes c^1, c^1. The f^1 and the e^1 of the third measure will be clear and vibrant; the preparation of the trill will be glided [*portée*], softened and formed by anticipation; then the trill itself will be reinforced with brilliance. The g^1 in the chest will take the covered timbre; the other notes, on the contrary, will take the open timbre. It is necessary to breathe before the word *aurora* in order to end the phrase with fulness. Moreover, tenderness, grace, and purity should characterize the expression of this phrase.

The choice of the shade in each effect is of the greatest importance. Certain singers have a very accurate feeling, but their expression, too concentrated, is not manifested enough, and their efforts leave us cold. Would it not be suitable to adopt the most vivid, the most encompassing [*méridionale*] shade, however without making it either grimacing or common?

From the varied use of the diverse elements which we have just studied the different styles arise.

Before passing on to the question of styles, we believe it necessary to point out some circumstances which often oblige the artist to modify the use of his means and the usual manner of his performance. They are: (1) the size and nature of the building; (2) the resources which he can put at the service of the composition; (3) the prejudices and the degree of intelligence of his listeners.

Firstly. One understands that in church less emotion is required than in the theater and more fervor [*onction*] and simplicity. One also understands that in a huge place the held tones, colors uttered in bulk, and pronounced contrasts are preferable to fine and detailed designs, and that these latter on the contrary have a better effect in a more confined room. Gluck would say regarding the opera *Orphée*, which he was composing for the theater at Parma: "*Large room, large note.*"

When one sings in a vast enclosure, one runs the double danger of stopping at that point, or of missing the result which one wishes to obtain. In order to place the performance into a correct relationship with the hall, the singer should increase the effects, not by the violence of the procedures, but by the intelligent choice of the means and the exact proportion of the details with the whole [*l'ensemble*]. It is especially in a huge room that it is important to use precisely the mechanism capable of producing the effect to which one aspires; for example: in order to lend to the curse of Edgardo its last degree of energy, it is necessary to resort neither to a strong thrust of the air, nor to a considerable volume of sound, but to the rending explosion of the consonant and to the clear timbre in all its brilliance. One should desire that the text appropriately present the occasion to apply this procedure. Take, as an example of the problem concerning us, the three versions following:

Donizetti: *Lucia*, Finale.

Edgardo.
e fe Ma - le - det - to
la foi A - na - the - me
1847: Per - fi - di - e
1872: Tra - di - tri - ce

It is the third [from either of the editions] which would be the most vigorous, and the second the coldest.

To explain in the same way the agitation of Assur:

> Fremer sento il cor nel petto
> (Rossini: Introduction from *Semiramide*.)

it is to the marked tones, to the jerks arising from the lungs, and not to any other procedure, that it is necessary to apply oneself.

Secondly. The same manner of rendering a piece could not suit singers gifted with different power, structure and resources.

Often even, for this reason, different artists will be led to present in the same composition so very many diverse shades included in the single emotion which propels it. This liberty is perfectly legitimate, always on the condition that the general agreement [*harmonie*] of the piece does not suffer from it.[67] We offer an example taken at random.

Rossini: *Tancredi*, Cavatina.

When a singer is not gifted with a voice powerful enough to fill a large hall, he should very carefully avoid resorting to exertion or exaggeration. These procedures, in place of increasing the means of the instrument, would have the effect of removing from it its charm and line

---

[67]One simple change of timbre suffices to change the logical meaning of a phrase. The following line:

"Je veux t'entretenir un instant sans témoin," (Racine)

can be addressed by a businessman to his client,
by a lover to his mistress,
by a conspirator to his accomplice,
by a criminal to his lawyer, etc., etc., and in these diverse cases, it will change tone and meaning, and will be able to express advice, love, terror or anxiety.

[*tenue*], of imparting to it a harsh and gutteral timbre, and in every case, of exposing it to serious attacks. Experience proves that the only means of increasing the projection [*portée*] of voices consists in reinforcing them with moderation and in nourishing them with a sparing and *continuous* current of air. Only a regular and sustained [*prolongée*] thrust can set the air contained in a large hall into motion and make it resonate.

Thirdly. We leave the responsibility of filling this paragraph to the intelligence of the artist. We will permit ourselves to say only that he should sacrifice as little as possible to false taste. The mission of the artist is to form the taste of the public, and not to warp [*fausser*] it by flattering it.

The various means which the study of the emotion puts at our disposal constitute more particularly the science of the dramatic singer; but these resources, added to the effects of the florid style, form a perfect cohesion [*ensemble*] which permits whoever possesses it to attain the greatest musical and dramatic effects. A pure and flexible organ, yielding to all the shades of the timbres, to all the needs of vocalization; a firm and correct syllabication; an expressive physiognomy; all these qualities joined to a soul which feels vividly the diverse emotions, to a musical sensitivity which understands all styles: such should be the unity offered by every singer who aspires to the first rank. *Outside of that, one could be no more than a respectable artist.*

CHAPTER V

THE VARIOUS STYLES

To the diverse styles of composition there correspond as many different styles of performance.

In 1723, Tosi recognized three kinds of styles: chamber style [*stilo di camera*], church style [*stilo di chiesa*], and theatrical style [*stilo di teatro*]. *Per il teatro* (Tosi always said), *vago e misto; per la camera, miniato e fiorito; per la chiesa, affetuoso e grave;* that is to say:

> For the theater, beautiful and varied;
>
> For the drawing-rooms [*salons*], polished [*fini*] and ornate;
>
> For the church, moving [*touchant*] and solemn.

Today when these styles are no longer as distinct as in the two past centuries, it is the nature of the composition which should determine the choice of style. If one takes into account the different characteristics which melodies can present, and the various methods of performing them, one finds that there are three principal styles from which all the others are derived, namely:

> The broad style, *canto spianato;*
>
> The florid style, *canto fiorito;*
>
> The dramatic style, *canto declamato*.

The broad style is not subdivided.

The *canto fiorito* can be divided into styles called *d'agilità, di maniera, di grazia, di portamento, di bravura, di forza, di slancio.*

The *declamato* style is divided into the serious and the comic. These names express the nature of the piece or the dominant characteristics of the performance. Thus, for example, the words *portamento, bravura, maniera,* indicate the principal role played in the first by the portamento, in the second by powerful passages, and in the third by graceful forms, etc.

1. RECITATIVES

Already, in the article on *Rhythm*, we have said that sometimes music rigorously follows the beat, and sometimes it frees itself from it. The first kind includes the measured pieces, to which are commonly given the name of *song* [*chant, canto*]. To the second kind belong the non-measured pieces which are called *recitatives*, from the Italian word *recitare*, which means to *declaim.*

The recitative is then a free musical declamation. One can distinguish two kinds of them: the spoken recitative [*recitativo parlando*] and the sung recitative [*recitativo instrumentale*]. In both cases, it has for its base the grammatic prosody, the laws of which it rigorously follows. Thus, it subordinates the values of the notes, those of the rests, the rate of the delivery and the accents to the prosodic length or brevity of the syllables, to the punctuation, in short, to the movement of the discourse. The application of this precept is absolute, and assumes the singer has a perfect understanding of the prosody of the language in which he is singing, and the knowledge of what he is saying. Only this knowledge can prevent him from displacing the accents, and from misrepresenting the meaning of the words by false inflections, or by badly placed pauses.

Spoken Recitative (*Recitativo parlante*).

The spoken recitative is reserved exclusively for comic opera.[68] It is syllabic, and approximates simple discourse, because it is spoken at the same rate [*en même temps*] as it is sung. The cantilena of this recitative is generally written for the *middle register* of the voice, and is delivered like comedy, with grace, verve and naturalness. The composer modulates from time to time in order to break the monotony of the same scale, and to better express all the varieties of the diction. The cantilena should be spoken as long as the same chord lasts, but as soon as the modulation is presented, it is necessary to gradually resume the intonation, in order to make the resolution of the chords perceptible. The moment of that reprise is almost always indicated by the dominant seventh, which the director at the keyboard [*maestro al cembalo*] or the basses should make heard in advance. Example: [A]

Mozart: *Don Giovanni*, Cavatina.

[68]See the recitatives in the *Barbiere di Siviglia*, the *Matrimonio segreto*, the *Cenerentola*, etc.

Since recitatives are, in general, only a kind of platitude, the artist has the right, without failing the composer, to change the melody of it; he can do so especially when the resolution of the chord would confuse his memory. He should, in that circumstance, boldly vary the cantilena, without departing from the scale in which he is singing and without touching on the dominant seventh chord, until the moment when the accompaniment sounds it. Then he will resolve his part on the major third of the chord which the regular resolution presents. That note, being a real note in several chords at the same time, removes the chance that he will find himself off-key [*hors du ton*]. The longest routine can only imperfectly make up for the [lack of] knowledge of harmony in the application of this rule. An example of a long declamatory speech in the same chord is found in "*Presto, va con costor*" from *Don Giovanni*.

The spoken recitative rarely permits fiorituras; the only ones generally permitted are the *grupettos*, and it is by them that one

terminates it. Example: [B]

Mozart:
Don Giovanni,
Recitative.
Don Giovanni.
so - lì sa-re-mo e là gio-jel - - lo mi-o ci spo-se-re-mo
e là gio-jel - - lo mi-o ci spo-se-re-mo
e là gio-jel - - lo mi-o

The appoggiatura also finds its place in the recitative, not as an ornament, but as a raising of the voice to express the tonic accent of smooth or transitory words followed by a pause. This raising always falls on the first of the two or three equal notes, according to the kind of word.

In the body of the phrases, one often substitutes the prolongation of the tone for the appoggiatura. In the two cases, the note which carries the long syllable should have a value at least double that of the short syllables. [C]

Capable singers take great care to introduce a certain variety in the form and in the movement of the cantilenas, that is to say that they avoid equal values, the return of rests at equal distances, the repetition of the same intervals and the symmetry of the accents. Examples:

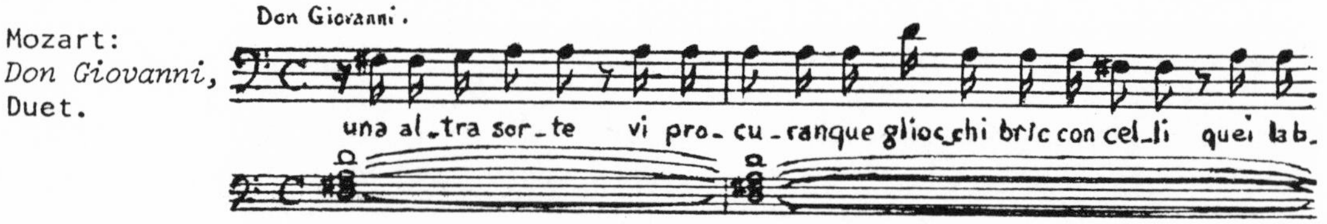
Mozart:
Don Giovanni,
Duet.
Don Giovanni.
una al-tra sor-te vi pro-cu-ranque glioc-chi bric con cel-li quei lab-

When the cantilena is frequently broken by intervals of the third, fourth and fifth, one makes it lyrical [*chantante*] by using the notes which are found between these intervals.

Accompanied Recitative (*Recitativo instrumentale*).

The accompanied recitative is *free* or *measured*. If it is measured, one will consider it as a fragment of an air, and it will need, as a consequence, to be submitted to the rules of that style. The accompanied recitative expresses noble and moving [*pathétiques*] sentiments, and should be sung with a broad and sustained style. Example:

*Rossini: *Otello*, Cavatina recit.

To the rules relative to prosody, we will add the following observations. The values of the notes and those of the rests often being determined only by the need to regularly divide the measure, they are only, to tell the truth, an indication of the movement which the thought should have. The true movement will arise from the meaning of the lines, and from that of the musical phrases. The two equal notes followed by a rest should never be said as they are written. The need to mark the accent requires, as much in the serious recitative as in the comic, that the first of the two notes be changed into an upper or lower appoggiatura, according as taste advises. In fact, sing scrupulously, note by note, the recitative which begins the scene from *Orpheus*:

> Sposa Euridice;
> (Gluck: *Orphée*.)

that of Donna Anna near her dying father:

> Ma qual mai s'offre, oh Dei;
> (Mozart: *Don Giovanni*.)

or else the scene of Sara:

> Chi per pietà mi dice;
> (Cimarosa: *Sacrifizio di Abraham*.)

and these three masterpieces of declamation would become unbearable after a few measures.

Sometimes one intercalates between the two notes a double appoggiatura, as was seen on page 121.

Although we cannot determine the particular use of the upper and lower appoggiaturas, we will nevertheless say that the lower appoggiatura is more moving [*pathétique*] than the upper.

In French recitative, instead of using the appoggiatura on the first of the two notes, one often prolongs the note which carries the long syllable, that is to say the first of the two notes; this custom undoubtedly results from the fact that in French the voice is dropped [*s'éteint*] on the feminine endings. Nevertheless, in many cases, the appoggiatura can be used with advantage. Example:

The instrumental recitative is ended well by ornaments which give a roundness to the musical thought. The color of these ornaments should always correspond to that of the recitative itself. Examples:

Rossini: *Otello*, Romance recitative.

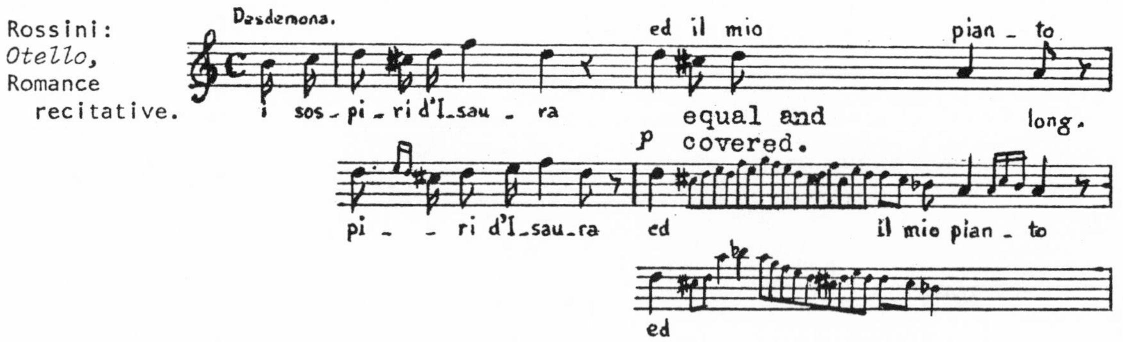

In the accompanied recitative the voice should remain entirely free of the accompaniment. That is why the chords are struck only when the voice has stopped, *and vice versa*. Examples:

Mozart: *Don Giovanni*, Duet recitative.

Mehul: *Joseph*, Aria Recitative.

Often, in order to free the voice, one joins chords which were separated by the recitative. Example:

Bellini: *Beatrice*, Cavatina Recitative.

When the melody is weak, one lends it a more fortunate turn by the use of passages, with the repetition of words, accents, colors of every kind; in short, everything can be permitted, provided one makes the feelings which one is expressing stand out with cohesion [*ensemble*] and in their true character. D

*In the following recitative, one can notice the changes of the notes and the repetition of the word *altri*.*[69]

---

[69]See, for the accompanied recitatives, the roles of Donna Anna in *Don Giovanni*, all the roles in *Guillaume Tell*, the scores of *Semiramide, Otello, Lucia;* the works of Gluck, the cantatas of Porpora, etc.

Bellini: *Beatrice*, Recitative.

Let us end this article by advising the student to place long pauses after the ritornellos which open the recitatives. The listener will be better prepared to listen, and his singing will be detached from everything which has preceded. It is moreover a means of recovering the calm which the sight of the public makes almost all artists lose at first. Some inhalations taken slowly, and saved until toward the last measures of the ritornello, have the effect of slowing the circulation, and of giving the respiratory apparatus and the larynx the freedom and the calm which they need.

2. ORDINARY AND BROAD SINGING (*Canto spianato*)

This style, the most noble of all, but also the least zesty

[*piquant*], because of the slowness of its movement and the simplicity of its forms, rests only on the shades of the emotion, and the variety of the musical chiaroscura. Here, nothing can substitute for the correctness of the intonation, the expression of the voice, the purity and the effects of syllabication, the musical coloring. This style has for its principal resources the clarity of the articulation and the various degrees of energy which it includes; the breadth and the equality of the voice; the agreement, the fusion or the delicacy of the timbres; the use of drawn out [*filés*] sounds in all varieties; the finest shades of dynamics, portamentos, the *tempo rubato*. The artist who has obtained this result, so difficult to obtain with only these resources, completing their effect with the *cantabili*, knows how to phrase all kinds of songs.

In the broad style of singing, which is the least favorable to ornamentation, the mechanical flexibility of the throat could not play the most important role. The superabundance of fiorituras, which smothers the effects of a broad and strict style under the mass of details, is the most difficult fault to pardon. Without being able to determine in a precise manner the ornaments which must be prohibited in this style, one can establish, in general, that it is necessary to exclude arpeggios and fiorituras composed of harsh and difficult intervals. The various appoggiaturas, the soft mordents and trills fit well here, and give the melody a certain relief which pleases. The other ornaments, when one has recourse to them, should be used with reservation, and should correspond, by the gravity of their movement and the softness [*douceur*] of their expression, to the breadth and the color of the style.

It goes without saying that, if it is necessary to forbid haste, passages performed in a brilliant and rapid manner, colors which are too detailed, it is equally necessary to avoid the heavy prolongation of notes followed by a pause, listlessness [*langueur*] in the endings, the abuse of the drawn out tones and portamentos, etc.

One of the distinctive characteristics of this style is that the vocal line should be constantly even and connected [*uni et lié*], which obliges that the passage from one tone to another be done without breaking [*expiration*], jerking or dryness. It is equally necessary that the changes of register be performed rather capably in order to remain unnoticed.

In this style the sustained [*filés*] tones play a very important role. *"*Una spianata di voce ben fatta,*" says Anna Maria Celloni, "*fa onore al discepolo ed al maestro, dimostrando tosto abbastanza l'ottima scuola.*" [A well done legato singing style does honor to both the student and the teacher, demonstrating quickly enough the best schooling.]* The student will thus profit from the opportunities to make a good hold on the clearest, most sonorous and firmest notes of his voice. The reader will recall the various procedures which we have indicated as aiding in the performance of sustained tones (see Part One). We will speak then only of the cases in which it is good to have recourse to it. One will sustain:

1. The note placed under the firmata, whether it is alone, or

followed by a passage. Examples:

*Bellini: *Norma*, Cavatina.

Donizetti: *Lucia*, Rondo.

2. Every note of arbitrary value placed at the beginning of a piece. Examples:

*Rossini: *Turco in Italia*, Duet.

Rossini: *Barbiere*, Duet.

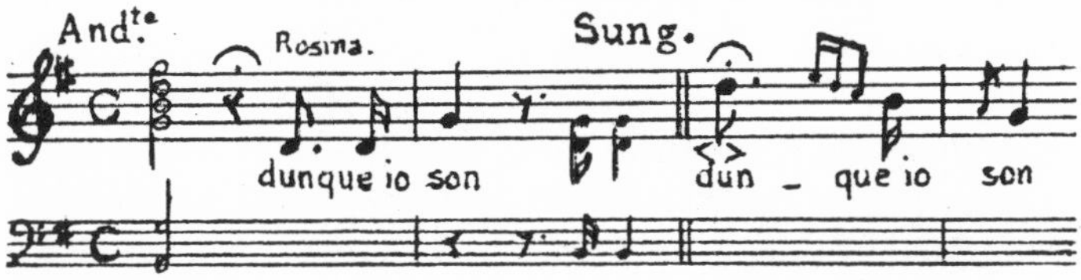

Cimarosa: *Sacrifizio*, Aria.

*Rossini: *Tancredi*, Duet.

*Rossini: *Mahomet*, Aria.

*Rossini: *Semiramide*.

*Rossini: *Semiramide*, Trio.

*Meyerbeer: *Robert le diable*, Aria.

3. Every note of sufficient value wherever it is offered in the *cantabile* styles.[70] Examples:

In these various cases, the length of the sustained tone is calculated according to the length of the passage which follows and the quantity of air necessary to this latter.

The need for gradation is made so imperatively felt in this style that one cannot attack the tones abruptly without offending the ear; those tones which require the most boldness should be given out with an intensification. [E]

Every singer gifted with a fine timbre of voice can also use the holds to depict by imitation the meanings of certain words expressing ideas of rest and of length: such are the words constancy, peace, calm, eternity, etc.

---

[70]These rules relative to the sustained tones are not exclusively applied to the *spianato* style: they extend to all the styles. One will want to remember this observation in the preceding paragraphs.

In the sixteenth and seventeenth centuries, musicians usually began with a *messa di voce* to immediately captivate the attention of the audience.

These rules for the spianato style, as we have just given them, are applied in all their vigor only to the *largo*. Examples of the *largo*:[71] [F]

The other *cantabile* movements, such as the *adagios*, the *maestosos*, the *andantes*, etc., although they retain a certain gravity from the *largo*, will be successively modified by aspects borrowed from the florid style, and alternately present long sustained notes and vigorous and showy passages.[72] [F]

The pure *largo* corresponds to touching [*pathétique*] feelings; the other mixed styles are better suited to noble and high feelings, whatever the emotion may be that they are expressing, gaiety, sadness, etc.

In the spianato style, it is necessary, for the very reason of the simplicity of the forms, that the artist stir [*remue*] the soul, under the pain of appearing level [*plat*] and listless [*languissant*]. *Also the clumsiness of the greater part of our singers, in this staid

---

[71]Ahi! di spirti turba immensa. (Handel: *Convitto di Alessandro*.)
Tutta raccolta in me. (Handel: *Nell'Ezio*.)
Fac me vere. (Haydn: *Stabat mater*.)
} *Collection de Chants classiques*, by L. B. C.

[72]The following pieces offer us examples of them:

"Casta diva."	*Norma.*
"Ahi! se tu dormi svegliati."	*Capuletti e Montecchi.*
"Idolo del mio cor."	*Romeo e Giulietta.*
"Bel raggio lusinghiero."	*Semiramide.*
"Per che non ho del vento."	*Lucia.*
"Qui la voce sua soave."	*Puritani.*
"In si barbara sciagura."	*Semiramide.*
"Sois immobile et vers la terre."	*Guillaume Tell.*
"Dove sono."	*Nozze di Figaro.*
"Ah non credea mirarti."	*Sonnambula.*

and delicate style, has obliged the composers to substitute for it, in their works, syllabic melodies with a decided rhythm. This system facilitates much the task of the performers, since, under the pretext of confronting the merit of a broad singing style, they spare the study of the shades, the chiaroscura, of a learned vocalization, the varieties of style, and finally that laborious and complete preparation which is the true education of the singer. For all that they are content to substitute the forcing of the voice and the exaggeration of the feelings: by that route one arrives at the decadence of the art.*

Many singers, I know, claim that the study of vocalization is completely useless for whoever aspires only to the use of the broad style. This assertion, more convenient than justified, is contrary to experience. The broad style becomes all the more easy when one has more completely shaped the organ to the difficulties of vocalization; let us say even that this suppleness is indispensable to whoever wishes to excell in the *largo* style. Heavy voices cannot attain perfection in any style. We could cite, if necessary, some artists who knew how to add a sustaining of the voice which left nothing to be desired to a most brilliant agility.

3. FLORID STYLE (*Canto fiorito*)[73]

This generic name includes every style which abounds in ornaments

---

[73]Garcia, Pellegrini, Mr. Tamburini, Miss Sonntag in 1829, Mrs. Damoreau.

and colors at the same time. The florid style permits the singer to display the fertility of his imagination, and to make the most of the sonority and flexibility of his voice. Here, as in the *spianato* style, one uses the *messa di voce, tempo rubato, portamento, dynamics,* in short, all the musical accents which were spoken of in the chapter on the art of phrasing. But the principal effect of this style is based on the passages. One should before all fit [*approprier*] them, by their harmony, their character and their performance, to the harmony and the character of the piece, as well as to the meaning of the words.

As the emotions variously modify the melodic means, and imparts to them different characteristics of grace, feeling, strength, etc., the florid style takes, for the very reason of those characteristics, the names of:

Canto di agilità.

Canto di maniera, which includes the *canto di grazia*
and the *canto di portamento.*

Canto di bravura, which includes the *canto di forza,*
the *canto di slancio*
and the *canto di sbalzo.*

These varieties are found sometimes isolated, sometimes joined in the same composition. Let us try to characterize each of them separately.

Canto di agilità.[74]

This style sparkles especially because of the rapid movement of the notes.

Roulades, arpeggios and trills abound in it. The treatment of the passages should be free [*franche*], the performance light, and the voice used sparingly. This style adapts perfectly to comic opera, to *allegro* movements of the gay airs, to the lively movements of the *rondos* and the variations.[75]

Canto di maniera (Synonym: Grace).[76]

One undoubtedly owes the creation of this style to singers whose voices lacked power, and whose organs, although capable of the

---

[74]Garcia, Messers Rubini, Tamburini, Madames Malibran, Demoreau, Sontag.

[75]Arias for Soprano: [G]

"Il dolce canto del Dio d'amore."	Rode: *Variations*.
"Non, je ne veux pas chanter."	*Billet de Loterie*.
"Idole de ma vie."	*Robert le Diable*.
"Plaisirs de la grandeur."	*Muette de Portici*.
Arias for Tenor:	
"Pria che spunti in ciel l'aurora."	*Matrimonio segreto*.
"Languir per una bella."	*Italiana in Algieri*.
"I tuoi frequenti palpiti."	*Niobe*.
Arias for Bass:	
"Sorgete, e in si bel giorno."	*Maometto*.
"Ah! si queste di mia vita."	*Zaira*.
Duet for Soprano and Tenor:	
"Amor possente nume."	*Armida*.
Duet for Soprano and Bass:	
"Di capricci."	*Corradino*.
Duet for Tenor and Bass:	
"All'idea di quel metallo."	*Barbiere di Siviglia*.

[76]Madames Pasta, Persiani, Mr. Velluti.

performance of difficult intervals, do not possess an extreme agility. In order to substitute for the most brilliant means of vocalization, the lively roulade, the arpeggio at full speed, the passages displayed on only one syllable, etc., these artists had recourse to ornaments composed only of little motives, to passages broken, arpeggiated and often cut by syllables, pauses and inflections. There is thus formed an elegant and delicate style whose turns receive the name of *modi di canto*. Their vocalization is, it is true, managed with art and well colored by the timbres and expression; but it is devoid of power, of fire [*brio*].

The *canto di maniera* corresponds to gracious feelings, whether the expression of them is gay or sentimental; that is why it is also named the *canto di grazia*. Only consummate singers can excell in it.

To these general considerations are added some precepts of detail consigned in part to the section on the art of phrasing. They are all inspired by the need for blending [the colors] and finesse [*le besoin de fondu et de fini*]. The tones which end the motives or members of phrases, when followed by a breath or a silence, will always be short and of the same degree of strength as the end of the preceding note. The final notes of the periods should be a little longer, but without a trailing off [*sans queue*].

After the silence required by the *breath* and the *half-breath*, after short [*quittées*] notes, or after an interrupted passage or *conduit*, it is necessary to resume the melody in the same timbre and the same degree of force as one had before the interruption, since the thought is only momentarily suspended and not changed. *Example:*

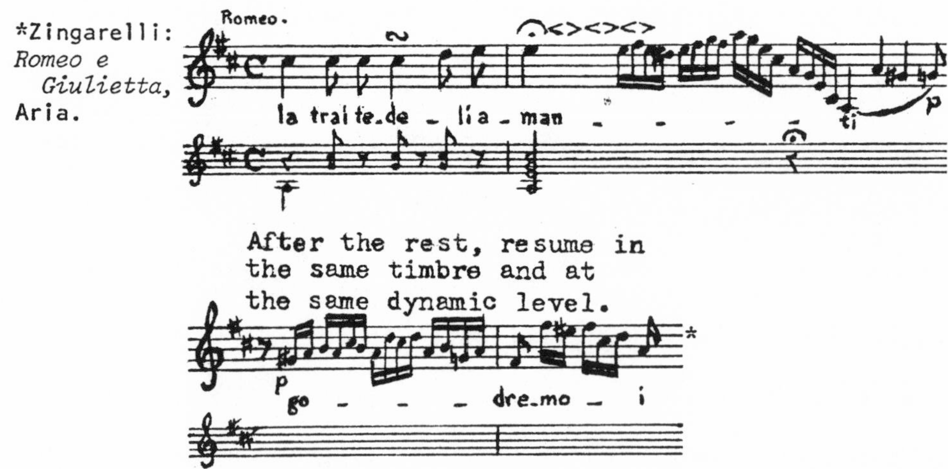
*Zingarelli: *Romeo e Giulietta,* Aria.
Romeo.
la trai te-de - li a - man - - - - ti
After the rest, resume in the same timbre and at the same dynamic level.
go - - - dre-mo - i

Let us also add some details relative to the development of the characteristics which this style includes. The phrases are colored by motives, by progressions, by inflections, rather than by phrase members. This is why one detaches by *half-breaths*, or by simple silences, all the little thoughts which comprise each phrase. The same artifice permits the preparation of the consonants and the giving of a certain finesse to each detail.[77]

The clear and the obscure, the soft and the loud, should be used always by well shaded gradations, and never in a brusque and hard manner. It is necessary that the notes be perfectly tied to each other, without any separation, any jerk to mark the passage of them. Bursts of the voice, dull sounds, harshly articulated consonants and the exaggeration of the effects will always be excluded from this delicate style.

The voice in the high and sustained tones should be softened to

---

[77]The miniature style [*canto miniato*], of which Tosi speaks for the chamber style, must undoubtedly have been obtained by these procedures.

the finest and most pleasant *pianissimo*. The mouth facilitates this pianissimo by half smiling.

One never swells [*renforce*] in descending graceful passages.

Repeated notes should be touched very lightly with the throat.

The mechanism of the *canto di maniera*, which includes delicacy and polish [*fini*] to a high degree, requires that one conserve the breath, that all the intervals be performed by supple movements of the organs, in place of being thrown by strokes of the chest; it is thus that one performs passages with difficult intervals, *soft mordents*, soft [or gentle] endings and melodies which are sung at the flower of the lips [*a fior di labbra*], as the Italians say, and other pieces of finely drawn character [*di mezzo carattere*].

When portamentos predominate, this style is named *canto di portamento*. In this style one often has recourse to lower appoggiaturas of all distances; the use of this means imparts softness [*douceur*] to the voice. Examples:[78]

Canto di bravura.[79]

The *canto di bravura* is nothing but the *canto di agilità*, only

---

[78]Romance.	"Assisa al pie d'un salice."	*Otello*, Rossini.
Cavatina.	"Il braccio mio."	Nicolini.
Cavatina.	"Di tanti palpiti."	*Tancredi*, Rossini.
Preghiera.	"Di calma o ciel."	*Otello*, Rossini.
Aria.	"Ombra adorata."	*Romeo e Giulietta*, Zingarelli.
Trio.	"Giovinetto cavalier."	*Crociato*, Meyerbeer.

[79]Garcia, in *Otello*, Madames Catalani, Malibran, Grisi.

with the addition of power and emotion. The artist can sing *di bravura* when he possesses a brilliant and full voice, a free and vigorous agility, boldness [*hardiesse*] and warmth. In this style [*genre*], the burst of the emotion is married to the richest ornamentation of the melody [*style*]: brilliant arpeggios, roulades, trills, portamentos, vivid colors, energetic accents, etc.

Bravura singing suits all brilliant and impassioned music.

This style requires that one reinforce the low notes of the descending passages. With women, the chest tones are the only ones which can satisfy this need of energy and power.

We believe we need to place here an observation borrowed in part from Lichtenthal.

The bravura style applied to the *agitato* includes one of the most impassioned movements in music, and demands not only some fire and abandon, but also a kind of exaltation and delirium. It is thus that one can express suffering, anger, jealosy and the other impetuous emotions with strength and truth. The accents, syncopations, rubato, the expressive timbres, some ornaments very appropriate to the words and performed with rapidity and the necessary strength, serve to depict the disorder and the spirit [*fougue*] of the various passions.

Examples: *Donna del Lago*, Trio;

Elisabetta, Duet between Elisabetta and Norfolk.

The *canto di bravura*, when it is dominated by large intervals, takes the name of *canto di slancio* [throwing style].

*After a recitative, it is in good taste [*de grande école*] to cut into a strong motive with a passage of bravura. Example:

Examples of bravura passages:

Distinctive (*caractérisés*), Popular Songs.

As national songs are essentially a part of the florid style, we will classify them in this paragraph. These songs are certainly those with the most distinctive melodies. I will say only a word about the style of the Spanish airs which are most familiar to me.

The Spaniard sprinkles his song with numerous mordents which attack the notes, and with frequent syncopations which displace the tonic accent, so as to add more piquancy to the effect by an unexpected rhythm. It is only at the end of the phrase that the voice coincides with the bass. The last syllable of the line does not fall on the strong beat of the last measure as in Italian, but on the last beat, that is to say, on the weak beat of the measure which precedes.

The colorings are vivid and strongly contrasted. All the final notes are short, except in the *polo*, in which the last note is long and shaky. In this latter style the voice takes on a melancholy aspect. The other styles are light, sensual [*voluptueux*] and flexible.

The final phrases of songs in this style nearly always end by throwing the voice onto a high and indecisive note resembling a little cry of joy. The Neapolitans use it equally; but the style of their songs differs less from the regular style than that of the Spanish melodies.

4. DECLAMATORY SINGING

Declamatory songs are nearly always monosyllabic; they exclude almost all vocalization. This style, created for the impassioned feelings, undoubtedly has recourse to the musical accents, but its principal effect rests upon the dramatic accent. The singer should, as a consequence, make everything converge to this end. The syllabication, the grammatical quality, the very well graduated strength of the voice, the timbres, the bold accents, the sighs, the expressive and unexpected transitions, and finally some appoggiaturas and portamentos, such are the elements to which he has recourse.

The diction should be not only correct [*juste*], but noble, lofty [*élevée*]; the affected, trivial and exaggerated forms are suitable only in parody and in comic caricatures [*buffi caricati*]. In order to excell in the dramatic style, it is necessary to have a soul of fire, a gigantic power; the actor should constantly dominate the singer.[80] But one should be careful to approach this style only with moderation and reserve, for it quickly exhausts the resources of the voice. Only the singer whose constitution is strong, but who, through a long practice of his art, has lost the freshness, the youth and the flexibility of the voice, should adopt it. The use of it is reserved for the final period of his talent.[81] "*Tutto quello che è di forza non è per li stessi mezzi che quello che è di grazia e di dolcezza.*" [All that which is strong is not of the same means as that which is graceful and sweet. -- Anna Maria Celloni.]

Spoken Style (Comic).

The spoken style is the soul of comic opera. This style is monosyllabic like the preceding, but of a completely opposite character. It requires that the words follow each other very rapidly and with a perfect clarity.[82]

---

[80]Mr. Duprez, Madame Schroeder Devrient.

[81]The role of Eleazar in *La Juive*, the operas of Gluck; the arias: *Rachel quand du Seigneur*, from *La Juive*; *Sois immobile et vers la terre*, from *Guillaume Tell*; *Quand renaître*, from *Guido et Ginevra*.

[82]To place the voice well and articulate well at the same time are two rare merits, but yet reconcilable and very necessary. We have the living proof of it in Mr. Lablache. We recall also that the glottis should, by means of a nourished breath and continuous and sonorous vibrations, prolong the tones as if they were not divided by words,

Here, still more than in serious declamation, the word and the intentions of the comedian should predominate.

In this style, the spirit and the comic verve are marvellously supported [*secondés*] by the agility of the vocal organs. Women and tenors could not be surpassed in it. When they possess these qualities, bass-baritones [*buffi cantanti*] make use of it to the greatest advantage.[83] The *buffo caricato* is the only one who speaks the song, and to whom agility is useless. He should be above all a comedian. One expects of him comic verve and witty jests, not elegance of voice.

Having arrived at the end of a thankless [*ingrat*] and laborious work, I do not deceive myself at all about what it leaves to be desired: I had understood beforehand the extreme difficulty of such a task. To precisely break down these successful [*heureux*] methods which accomplished singers encounter most often just by their instinct for the art, and to reduce them to a system to place them within the reach of all, this is what I have attempted, what I did not hope to accomplish.

It is enough for me to think that I have perhaps offered to the public the elements of a useful work, and that some questions raised in this method will call the attention of some of the most capable masters to resolve them. I have outlined [*ébauché*] the work; science and talent will complete it [*y mettront la dernière main*].

---

while the articulators impart to the notes the movement of the consonants. (See for example note 26, page 30, Part Two.)

[83]Garcia, Pellegrini, Tamburini, Ronconi.

In this second part, as in the first, one should transpose the examples according to the tessitura [*diapason*] of the voices.

EXAMPLES OF FINAL CADENCES

s'in - - - vo - - - lò fe - - - - del - - - - tà
no non v'è pie - ta no a - me - rò che te
ca pa - - ce di fren no il cor vam - mi on deg - - gian - - do il cor
non v'è pie - tà non v'è pie - - tà
che l'e gal non ha tan - - ta in - fe - - - - del - tà
è un ter - ri - bi - le guer - rier d'ar - - dir m'ac - cen - - de il cor
vo - - la a tri - on - far e s'in - - vo lo
scio - - gli leg - gie - - ro il piè ca - da il ti - ran - no re - gno d'a - mor
vo - - lo a tri - - - - on - far sen - - to in - fiam - mar - - - si il cor
vo - - lo a tri - - on - - far sol - - ca l'im - men - - - so mar
li - be - ro ca - cia - - tor sen - - to in - fiam - mar - - - si il cor
no il cor non hà il cor non hà ah! che mai sa - rà che mai sa - rà
no il cor non hà il cor non hà ah! che mai sa - rà che mai sa - rà
no il cor non hà il cor non hà ah! che mai sa - rà che mai sa - rà

si fe - li - ce o - gnor fe - li - ce o - gnor
del do - lor del do - lor
bar - ba - ro do - lor si do - lor
si la no - bi - le mer - cè la no - bi - le mer - cè
si di pa - ce a - mor di pa - ce a - mor
si col su - o can - tar col su - o can - tar
a - do - ra - bi - le bel - tà a - do - ra - bi - le bel - tà
e - i ne in - vi - ta a ri - de - re e scher - zar ne in - vi - ta a ri - de - re scher - zar
no per mè non v'è mag - gior pe - nar no non v'è mag - gior pe - nar
e - i ne in - vi - ta a ri - de - re scher - zar ne in - vi - ta a ri - de - re scher - zar
dal pia - cer bal - zan - do và dal pia - cer bal - zan - do và
non per mè non non per mè non v'è
dal cor già s'en và dal cor s'en và
si scher - zan - do và scher - zan - do và
già crol - lan - do và crol - lan - do và
già crol - lan - do và crol - lan - do và
ah! scher - zan - do và scher - zan - do và
dal pia - cer sal - tan - do và sal - tan - do và

è un tra - di - tor v'in - gan - ne - rà è un tra - di - tor v'in - gan - ne - rà
no per me non è per me non è
no pia - cer no maggior non v'è mag - - gior non v'è
non pia - cer mag - gior non v'è mag - - gior non v'è
si fe - - li - - ci - - tà fe - - li - - ci - - tà
no per me non v'è per me non v'è
no per me non v'è per me non v'è
vam - mi on - - deg - - gian - - do il cor vam - mi on - deg - gian - - do il cor
vam - - mi on - - deg - gian - - do il cor on - - deg - gian - - do il cor
ah i tan - ta m - a fe - li - - ci - tà ah tan - - ta mi - a fe - li - - ci - tà
vor - - rei vor - rei con tè res - tar con tè con tè res - tar
deh! vie - ni vie - ni sul mio cor deh vie - ni vie - ni sul mio cor
vor - rei con tè con tè res - - tar vor - rei con tè con tè res - tar
fra le pal - me a tri - - on - far fra le pal - me a tri - on - far
fra le pal - me a tri - on - far fra le pal - me tri - on - far
si sa - rai sa - rai sa - rai mio cor pa - - go sa - rai mio cor
pa - - go sa - rai sa - rai mio cor pa - go sa - ra - i sa - rai mio cor

pa - go sa - rai_i sa - rai_i mi_o cor pa - go sa_ra_i sa - ra_i mi_o cor
pa - go sa - ra_i sa - ra_i mi_o cor pa - go sa_ra_i sa - ra_i mi_o cor
di quà di là vo_la il pen_sier di quà di là di quà di là vo_la il pensier vo_la il pen_sier di quà di là di quà di là
ci di nuo_vo an cor an cor ver - ra an - cor ver - ra
vo - la il pen_sier di quà di là vo - la di quà di là
va di quà di là di quà di là
già fre - men - do và fre_men_do va fre_men_do và
non per me non vè per me per me non vè
vo - la il pen - sier di quà di là il pen - sier di quà di là
che fe - li - ci - tà fe - li - ci - tà
non per me per me non vè pie - ta non vè pie_ta
ah! v'in - gan - ne - rà v'in - gan - ne - rà
ah! v'in - gan - ne - rà v'in - gan - ne - rà
ah! v'in - gan - ne - rà v'in - gan - ne - rà

EXAMPLES OF ORGAN POINTS FOR ONE AND TWO VOICES

In order to avoid the voice being covered by the accompaniment, the singer will begin only a few moments after the chords have been struck.

ritard.
guer - ra
fu nes - ta_no
es tre - mo
guer - ra
pal - pi_to
al l' ar - mi
vie - ni
in_ciam - po
che do - lor
mi fâ ge_lar
che do_lor
sen_za di tè che mai che ma - i fa_rò
tu - o bel cor
fol - le ar_dor
del te - ne_ro mio cor
o diar
o diar - mi al_lor
o diar - mi al_lor
in tal do_lor
o diar - mi ah non o diar - mi al_lor
o diar - mi al_lor

d'af_fan no io d'af_fan_no mo_ri_rò
per_ples so il cor
ed a_mis_tà
i'ado_ra to mio ben
il mi o va_lor
mi tra di
del mio cor
do ve an drò
mo ri_rò
ah! la vin_ce_rò
per me ah! si per me can_giò
f
p
mf
ah! io mo_ri_rò
rall.
fe del_tà
e_ter_no e_ter no è il do_lor
e_ter no il do_lor
can giò ah! can_giò
mor_rò di do_lor
morrò di do_lor
amor ci con du_rà
implo ro implo ro_gnor

ah! can_giò
e_ter - - - - - - no il do_lor e - - ter - no il do_lor
sem - - - - - pre sem - - - - - - pre pe_nar per tè
bril - - - - - - la il guardo e bal - - - - - - za il cor
ris_ve - - - - - - glia' nel pen_sier
e vo - la al ciel vo - la vo - - - - - - la al ciel
on deg - - - - - - gia nel se - no on deg - gia nel se - - - - - - no il cor
ser - - ban no
o mag gio e fe - - - - - - del tà
f
f
bril - - - - - - la il guar_do e bal - - - - - - za il cor
rit.
l'è_gua - - - - - - le non si dà
ta_cio cor mo
ta - - - - - - cio cor sa_ra - - - - - - men cru_del

sen - - - - to sen - to lan_guir
ah del suo do_lor
sen - - - - - - to lan_guir
e a_mor
sen - - - - - - to lan_guir
m'incal - - - - - - za o_gnor
l'ar - - - - - - mi d'a_mor
on deg - - - - - - gia il mar
ah! l'es - - - - - sermo_bil mo_bil e in_fe_del
che di ra
che fa ro
p
Very long.
te - - - - co o_gnor
conten - - - - - ta con_ten - - - - ta con_ten_ta io mo_ri_ro
va - - - - - cillare fan - - - - - no il mio cor
var - - - - - ca i mon - - - - - - tic il mar
ca_gion del fier del fier do_lor

l'in_cer - - - - - to cor ra - - - - - - pi_do spa_ri
non in_dug_giar ah! spa_ri
ah! sen_za po_ter mo_rir
sen - - - - - - - - - - - - - - - za po_ter mo_rir
ah: il se_gre_to del mio cor
ah: di gio_ja pal - - - pi_tar
ah: ah di gio_ja pal_pi_tar
e gra - - - - - - - - - to o gnor con_te
non vi_di più
del valor del va_lor il fie - - - - - - - ro ar_dor
nol spe_ra_re non tar dar
che do - - lor che do - - lor
in fe - - - - - - del_ta qua - - - - - - le or_ror

a Tempo.
ritard.
o - diar - - - - - - - mi al - lor non o - diar - - mi al - lor non o - diar - - mi al - lor
o - diar - - - - - - - - mi al - lor non o - diar - - mi al - lor non o - diar - mi al - lor
ah! che gio - - - - - - va il pal - - pi - tar
ah! che gio - - - - - - - va il pal - - pi - tar
Voice.
longue
l'es - - - - - - - - - - - - ser mo - bil ed in - fe - del
Clarinetti
Accomp.
ah la fiam - - - - - ma la fiam - - - - ma del tuo cor
ah la fiam - - - - - ma la fiam - - - - ma del tuo cor
perdon ah! ah!
perdon si - gnor per - don
ah! perdon del mio fal - lir si - gnor per - - don
ah! perdon del mio fal - lir si - gnor per - - don
sem - pre con te res - tar sem - - pre sem - - pre con tè sem - pre con tè res - tar
sem - pre con te res - tar sem - - pre sem - - pre con tè sem - pre con tè res - tar
e - ter - no e il do - lor
e - ter - no e il do - lor

Very connected.

il cor non ha non ha

il cor non ha non ha

tro_var pie_ta pie _ ta

pie_ta tro_var tro _ var pie _ ta

e fa spe_rar e fa spe _ rar

e fa spe_rar e fa spe _ rar

e fa sperar e fa spe _ rar

rall.

il ca - - - - - - - - - - pi_ra il ca - pi _ ra

il ca - - - - - - - - - - pi_ra il ca - - pi _ ra

a - - - - - - - - - - - men a - - - - - men

a - - - - - - - - - - - men a - - - - - men

Canto.

di gio - - - - - - - - - - ja pian - - - - -

Accomp.

- - ge - ra pian - ge - ra pian_ge_ra

Until now we have presented only some isolated precepts; we have enumerated the diverse elements of which the performance is composed: we are going to examine these parts in their relationship to the whole. In order to know profoundly all the resources of a scholarly practice, it would be necessary to carefully analyze a series of masterpieces, under the direction of a consummate artist; the able master, we do not claim to replace him here. In the indications which accompany the pieces, offered to the students for study, we do not hope to always determine the best means of rendering the melody, nor even to completely expose our personal manner of feeling it. We seek only to make understood by some examples how the student can apply the different principles posed in this method, and in what attitude [*disposition d'esprit*] he should approach the study of any piece whatever.

Abraham has left to go to carry out the order which he has received, to immolate his son. Sara, whom the poet supposes has been warned of his misfortune, looks for Isaac everywhere; the following piece includes the eloquent depiction of her torments.

The most dangerous pitfall [*écueil*] in the expression of energetic feelings is exaggeration or triviality; one avoids above all *this last fault*, by setting off by the purity and perfect correctness of style what the expression would have of excessive simplicity and vulgarity.

Cimarosa: *Sacrifizio d'Abraham*, Scene and Aria for soprano. Poetry by Metastasio.

Very accentuated portamentos. In this passage one cannot show too much power of voice and articulation.
Slow.
Sigh.
Strong Voice.
forte.
ff
piano.
Sigh of extreme anguish.
m.forte.
forte.
ah! l'in no_cen_te già spi_rò for_se l'al_ma in man del pa_dre ah forse oh! di_o che dolor
a tempo.
Tears and desolation.
Extremely legato.
breath.
Mordant which begins the note.
Slight rall.
Anxiety.
chi mi con_so_li non si tro_va per me
almen di tan_ti al_meno tor_nar ve
Precise and short words.
All°.
A kind of faint.
Slow.
forte.
sostenuto.
piano.
Anxiety.
des_si! ec_co_ne un si cer_chi chie_da_si non ho cor pas_to_ri ah!
Soft mordent, slow.
Slow.
Voice full and commanding.
tre_mo d'ascol_tar la rispos_ta ah! perche ma_i si con_fu_si tor_na_te dove A
Prolonged note.
Prolonged.
piano.
Light.
bram? che ve_de_ste? oh! Di_o par_la_te.

Release of air to end this note which should be very long.

Release of air.

ARIA. All° agitato.

Ah! parla_te! ah! par_la_te,

Ah! par_la_te! ah! par_la_te,

p cresc. p cresc. p

Full voice, very energetic portamentos.

Example of *tempo dérobé*.

Slight variant of measure 8.

deh! par_la_te che for_se ta_cen_do men pie_to_si

deh! par_la_te che for_se ta_cen_do men pie_to_si

p

The reply to measures 15 and 16, more accented and slightly varied.

piano. R. ½ Ath.

più bar_ba_ri sie_te deh! par_la_te che for_se ta_cen_do men pie_to_si più bar_ba_ri

B B B B

più bar_ba_ri sie_te deh! par_la_te che for_se ta_cen_do men pie_to_si più bar_ba_ri

Strong voice.

The stress of the note g^2 should arise principally from the preparation of the consonant [b].

sie_te men pie_to_si più bar_ba_ri sie_te

sie_te men pie_to_si più bar_ba_ri sie_te

This little note taken without portamento.

Sombre timbre, but sparkling.

Soft, pleading voice.

piano. p < cresc. forte. Br. piano

ah! v'in_ten_do ta_ce_te ta_ce_te non mi di_te che il fi_glio mo_ri non mi

ah! v'in_ten_do ta_ce_te ta_ce_te non mi di_te che il fi_glio mo_ri non mi

This phrase member more accentuated than at measures 29 and 30.
mf
piano.
f
Release of air before and after the note.
di - te che il fi - glio mo - ri h!ah! deh! par - la - te che for - se ta - cen - - do
Extend the note gb2.
Lively.
Extend the voice.
Extend the voice.
men pie - - to - si piu bar - ba - ri sie - - te men pie - to - si piu bar - bari sie - te oh
These two 32nd notes e2 and f2, slow and equal.
Messa di voce as much as possible.
The note f1 very full.
Declaimed.
piano.
p
Di - o par - la - te par - la - - te ah v'in - ten do ta ce te ta - ce - te non mi di - te che il fi - glio mo -
Full voice.
Sombre timbre.
Soft, marked.
Variant of measures 49 and 50.
One may accentuate the first, second, or fourth note of each beat.
piano.
- ri deh par - - la - te che for - se ta - cen - do men pie - - to - si piu bar - ba - ri
Aspirate the attack of the f2.
Increase the accent.
Variant.
Variant: increase of accent.
Variant: slight rall.
Sustained tone.
Voice covered and agitated.
Still piano
Jerky tones.
piano
sie - te oh Di - o par - la - te oh Di - o ta - - ce - - te ah v'in - ten - do ta - ce - te ta -

Prolong the voice.

Sob. Sob.

forte.

_ ce _ te non mi di te che il fi _ glio mo _ ri non mi di _ te che il fi _ glio mo _ ri no non mi di _ te che il fi _ glio mo _

_ ce _ te non mi di _ te che il fi _ glio mo _ ri non mi di _ te che il fi _ glio mo _ ri no non mi di _ te che il fi _ glio mo _

The whole phrase at full voice.

_ ri che il fi _ glio mo _ ri che il fi _ _ glio mo _ ri

_ ri che il fi _ glio mo _ ri che il fi _ glio mo _ ri

f p *> p* *fp* *fp* *f*

fp *fp* *fp*

These notes in chest voice and well held, *rinforz.*

piano. Half breath after portamento. Clear timbre.

col canto.

Slow preparation, smooth and gradually accellerated.

So che spi _ ra quell' os _ _ tia si ca _ _ _ _ ra,

So che spi _ ra quell' os _ _ tia si ca _ _ _ _ ra,

p

With tenderness.

a tempo. *piano.*

piano. *cres*

Increasing anxiety.

so che spi _ ra quell' os _ tia si ca _ ra veg _ _ go il san _ gue che tin _ _ ge quell'

so che spi _ ra quell' os _ tia si ca _ ra veg _ _ go il san _ gue che tin _ _ ge quell'

p

In order to express this outburst of grief in all its energy, the mind should be struck with all the nuances of fear and horror which are connected to the idea being expressed by the words.
piano cresc.
piano cresc.
forte.
ff
Beside herself.
a - ra sen - to il fer - ro che il sen le fe - ri deh par -
dim. dim. f dim. dim.
f cresc.
Heart-rending grief.
la - te che for - se ta - cen - do men pie - to si piu bar - ba - ri sie - te ah! ta - ce - te v'in - ten - do v'in - ten - do veggo, il
Exhausted, fainting away.
ff
fi - glio veggo il san - gue, veggo il fer - ro che il sen le fe - ri gia spi - ra oh
Exclamation of poignant grief.
Pronounce [y] as in French, but however without closing the lips.
rall. dimin.
Pleading voice.
p
With fright.
Du - o! deh par - ta - te ta - ce - te v'in - ten - do
Di - o!
non mi di - te che il fi - glio mo - ri non mi di - te che il fi - glio mo -

p
cresc.
ri ah! par - la te che for - se ta - cen - do men pie -
f
p
f
p
cresc.
p
rall.
to - si piu bar - ba - ri sie - te oh Di - o par - la - te oh Di - o ta -
Concentrated voice, marked tones.
a Tempo.
Prolonged voice.
ce - te, ha! v'in - ten - do ta - ce - te ta - ce - te non mi di - te che il fi - glio mo - ri no no no non mi
Perform the final cadences brilliantly and vigorously.
di te che il fi - glio mo - ri no no no non mi di te che il fi - glio mo - ri non mi
di - te che il fi - glio mo - ri non mi di - te che il fi - glio mo - ri che il fi - glio mo - ri.

Carolina, the daughter of a rich merchant, has been asked in marriage, at the moment when she has just secretly married Paolino, an employee of her father. At the point of fleeing with his wife, Paolino tells her of the plans he has made to assure their withdrawal, and seeks to overcome her scruples by the keenest tenderness and the softest persuasion.

A gracious and tender voice, ornaments and accents imitative of the delicate or vigorous nuances: such are the means which will give to this admirable piece its true color and will make evident all the charm of it.

Cimarosa: *Matrimonio segreto*, Aria for tenor.

piano.
piano.
ra sor_ti_re_mo pian pia_ni_no per la por_ta del giar_di_no tut_ta pronta una ca_
ra sor_te_re_mo pian pia_ni_no per la por_ta del giar_di_no tut_ta pronta u_na ca_
f
p
forte.
mezzo voce.
roz_za la da noi si tro_ve_ra la da noi si tro_ve_ra chiu_si in quel_la il vet_tu_
roz_za la da noi si tro_ve_ra la da noi si tro_ve_ra chiu_si in quel_la il vet_tu_
piano.
mezza forte.
crescendo.
forte.
ri_no per schi_var qua lunque in top_po per schi_var qua lunque in top_po i ca_val_li di ga_
ri_no per schi_var qua lunque in top_po per schi_var qua lunque in top_po i ca_val_li di ga_
fp
fortissimo.
Falsetto.
Chest.
piano.
Tenderly.
cresc.
lop_po sen_za po_sa cac_cie_rà sen_za po_sa cac_cie_
lop_po sen_za po_sa cac_cie_ra sen_za po_sa cac_cie_
fp
p
f
piano.
Caressing voice.
piano.
crescendo.
ra da una vecchia mia pa_rente buo_na don_na e as_sai pie_to_sa ce n'andre_mo ca_ra
ra da una vecchia mia pa_rente buo_na don_na as_sai pie_to_sa ce n'andre_mo ca_ra

Wavy tones.

spo_sa e stare_mo che ti la ca - ra spo_sa ca - - - ra spo_sa e sta_re - - mo che_ti

spo_sa e sta_re_mo che ti la ca - - ra spo - sa ca - - ra spo - sa e sta re - mo che ti

fp

Falsetto. ritard. . a tempo.

la e stare - - - - - - - - - mo che_ti la e staremo che_ti la e sta_re_mo cheti

la e sta_re - - - - - - - mo che - ti la e sta_re_mo che_ti la e sta_ra - mo che - ti_

Contained emotion.
Strict time.

All.° vivace

piano.

la e sta_re_mo che_ti là

Co_me poi s'a vra da fa_re pen_se_

la e sta_re - mo che_ti la

Co_me poi s'a vra da fa_re pen_se_

All.° vivace.

f p

The accents on the weak beats very marked.
Voice prolonged.

piano.

remo a men_te cheta

spo_sa ca_ra sta pur lie_ta che l'a_mor ci assis_te_

remo a men_te cheta

spo_sa ca_ra sta pur lie_ta che l'a_mor ci as_si - ste_

f p

The voice prolonged on these little phrases.

piano.

forte.

_rà spo - - sa ca_ra stà pur lie_ta stà pur lie_ta che l'a_mo_re che l'a_

ra spo - sa ca_ra sta pur lie_ta sta pur lie_ta che l'a_mo_re che l'a_

f p f p f

cresc.
These notes well marked.
mor ci as_sis _ _ te ra ci assis_te _ ra ci assis_te _ rà
dol.
The voice very sustained.
piano.
Pria che spunti in ciel l'au_ro_ra ca_ra spo_sa sen_ti be_ne
sorti
The voice very sustained and constant crescendo.
Full voice.
re_mo pian pia_ni_no per la por_ta del giar_di_no che _ _ ti che _ _ ti a len _ _ to pas _ _ so scen _ de_
_ re _ _ mo fi _ no ab_bas _ so che nes _ sun ci sen _ ti _ rà che nes_sun ci sen_ti _ rà pronta
dimin.
piano.
pp
cresc.
pronta la ca_rozza la da noi si tro _ ve _ _ rà la da noi si tro_ve _
f
cresc.

piano.
cresc.
mezzo forte.
-rà scen-de-re-mo sor-ti-re-mo sor-ti-re-mo pia-no
-ra scen-de-re-mo sor-ti-re-mo sor-ti-re-mo pia-no
p
cresc.
f
Sustained tone.
Ad libitum.
Portamento.
pia-no a pas-so len-to che nes-sun ci sen-ti-ra spo-sa ca-ra
a piacere.
pia-no a pas-so len-to che nes-sun ci sen-ti-ra spo-sa ca-ra
cresc.
col canto.
primo tempo.
piano.
sta pur lie-ta che l'a-mor ci as-sis-te-rà sor-ti-re-mo pian pia-
sta pur lie-ta che l'a-mor ci as-sis-te-ra sor-ti-re-mo pian pia-
p
crescendo.
piano.
-ni-no per la por-ta del giar-di-no pian pia-ni-no pian pia-ni-no pronta pron-ta la ca-
-ni-no per la por-ta del giar-di-no pian pia-ni-no pian pia-ni-no pronta pron-ta la ca-
cresc.
crescendo.
f
a piacere.
Wavy tones.
The preparation of the trill should be soft, smooth, and gradually accellerated.
lento.
con brio.
Release the eb2 lightly.
Breath.
-roz-za la da noi si tro-ve-ra spo-sa ca-ra sta pur
a piacere.
-roz-za la da noi si tro-ve-ra spo-sa ca-ra sta pur
col canto.

Soft.
Breath.
Quickly and with force.
1º Tempo.
lie - - - - ta che l'a - - mor ci as - sis - te - ra
che l'a - mor ci as - - sis - te - rà che l'a - mor ci as - - sis - te -
- rà ci as - sis - te - rà ci as - sis - te - rà ci as - - sis - - te - - rà ci as - -
- sis - - te - - rà ci as - sis - te - rà ci assis - te - rà.
sf

The subject of the following piece is too well known to require giving an analysis of it.

Crescentini: Aria for mezzo-soprano inserted into *Romeo e Giulietta* by Zingarelli.

Recitativo.
forte.
Prolonged tones.
Tone sustained with inflections.
Ma che va_le il mi - - o duol! mia bel_la spe_me io ti sen_to mi chia mi a seguir_ti fra
Ma che va - - le il mio duol! mia bel_la spe_me io ti sen_to mi chiami a se - guir - ti fra
p
Resolutely.
l'om_bre eb_ben, m'aspet _ ta, ti se_gui _ ro
l'ombre eb _ ben, m'as _ pet _ ta, ti se_gui _ ro
cresc. f
rinf.
se a te compagno in vi - ta non mi vol - - - - - - le la sor _ te te_co m'unis - - ca al_
se a te com_pagno in vi _ ta non mi vol - - - - - - le la sor_te te_co m'u_nis - - ca al -
f
f
dim.
p
And.te sostenuto.
_ men pie_to - - sa mor_te.
_ men pie _ to _ sa mor_te
p
p
mf
With animation.
Tranquil - lo io son, fra po_co te_co sa_ro mia vi_ta
Tranquillo io son, fra po_co te - co sa_ro mia vi_ta
p

Slow.
accogli intan_to mia spe_me, a - - - - - - ni_ma mi_a, accogli in_tanto questo ch'io per
ac_cogli in_tanto mia spe_me, a - - - - - - - ni_ma mi_a, ac_cogli in_tan_to ques_to ch'io per te
Slow.
RONDO. Andte mosso.
ver_so ul_ti - - mo pian_to.
ver_so ul_ti_mo pianto.
Largo assai.
With verve (exaltation).
Ombra a_dora_ta as_pet_ta, te_co saro in_di - vi_so, nel for_tuna - - to e_
Om_bra a_do_ra_ta as_pet_ta, te_co saro in_di - vi_so, nel for_tu_na_to e_
With power and warmth.
Voice sustained (étendue).
- li - - so a - vra con_ten_to il cor. ombra a_do_ra_ta as -
- li - - so a_vra con_ten_to il cor. ombra a_do_ra_ta as -
Soft. cresc. cresc.
- pet_ta te_co sa_ro in_di vi_so, nel for_tu_na_to e_li - - so a_vra con_
pet_ta te_co sa_ro in_di - vi_so, nel fortuna_to e_li - - so a_vra con_

cresc.
ten _ to a _ vra con _ ten _ to il cor a _ vra con _ ten _ to il cor
Half voice.
Lightly.
Full voice.
La, trai fe _ de _ li a _ man _ ti ci ap _ pres _ ta a _ mor di _ let _ ti, go _
The entire organ point should be performed on one breath, taken before the syllable man; but this liberty should remain unnoticed by the audience.
breath.
dre _ mo i dol _ ci is _ tan _ ti, la, trai fe _ de _ li a _ man _ ti go _
rinforz.
dre _ mo i dol _ ci is _ tan _ ti di più in _ no _ cen _ ti af _ fet _ ti e
Full
and sonorous voice.
l'e _ co a noi d'in _ tor _ no ri _ suo _ ne _ ra d'a _ mor, ri _ suo _

rinf.
dim.
Graciously.
- - - - - - - - ne - ra ri - suo-ne ra d'a - mor.
- - ne - ra ri - - - suo - - ne ra d'a - mor.
f
ombra a-do-ra-ta as-pet-ta te - co sa-ro in-di - - vi-so nel for-tu-na - to e - -
ombra a - do - ra - ta as - pet - ta te - co sa ro in-di - - vi-so nel for-tu-na - to e - -
p
cresc.
forte.
Soft.
- li - so a-vra con-ten-to a - - vra con - ten - to il cor, a - vra conten-to il
- li - so a - vra con - ten - to a - - vra con - ten - to il cor, a - vra con-ten-to il
rf
cresc.
f
cor, a - vra con-ten-to il cor, a - - vra con-ten-to il cor, a - - -
cor, a - vra con-ten - to il cor, a - - vra con-ten - to il cor, a
p
sfz
f p fp
- vra con - - teu - - to il cor.
vra con - ten - to il cor

The aria which follows belongs to the style of the past century and offers a remarkable example of it. I got it from Giovanni Batista Velluti who is the only person today who possesses the secrets of that extinct school.

G. B. Velluti, the last famous Italian sopranist, was born in Monterone in the province of Ancona in 1781. He lives retired near the banks of the Brenta.

Morlacchi: *Teobaldo ed Isolina*, Aria.

Slight exhalation.
Open timbre.
Light note and syllable.
Rapid appoggiatura performed without portamento.
Smooth, equal and slightly covered notes.
After the accompaniment an inhalation of surprise.
Inhale.
Sound the [n] on the note f. This syllable light.
h!ma allor_e ra fe_li_ce
or tris_tae so
pianiss.
la
forse a me
for_se a me pe_n_sa
After the voice.
Melancholy voice.
Ringing.
Sustain the voice over all the notes.
p
e il su_o do lo
rall.
con_so_la
Laughing physiognomy. Outburst of the soul. Clear timbre.
Ringing.
Pharynx contracted.
ca_ro suo_no lu__sin
And^te mosso.
ghier dolce o gnor mi scen__de al cor
Soft mordent.
rinf.
Tones imitating an echo.
smorzando.
dol_ce o_gnor mi scen_de al cor tu ri
rinf.
de al cor tu ri
Inhalation after the portamento.
col canto.
cresc.
f
p
Echo.
Pharynx contracted.
dolce.
cresc.
chia mi al mi o pen_sier i pia cer d'un cas___to a_mor quel bel di che ci ra-
cer d'un cas__to a_mor
p f p f

Mouth laughing.
Pharynx contracted.
Slight movements of the larynx.
Portamento arpeggio.
Sob, jerky inhalation.
Make a slight exhalation before the [d].
Sob, jerky exhalation.
Noisy exhalation.
Exhalation.
pi de sua pu-ra vo - - - lut-ta h! Do - ve an-do h! Do - ve an-do do - h! ve an-
sempre
immer
secondando
den Gesang
il canto
unterstützend
Held.
Strong. 6 fast notes.
Breath.
piano.
Slow.
Exhalation.
Exhalation.
Exhalation.
rall.
do do ve ando mio ben quel di h! a - h! mai più h! a - h! mai più a - - h! mai più no no mai più ri-tor-ne-
colla parte
sempre secondando il canto.
Release the tone with an exclamation.
Pharynx contracted.
Tone imitating an echo.
adagio.
Inflections.
Prepare the consonant [m] without breathing.
Inhale.
ra mai più mai più a-h! mai più ri - tor - ne - ra a - - - h! mai più no non mai
a tempo.
forte
più ri - tor - ne - ra

Assur, devoured by ambition and arrogance, pursues with an implacable hatred the one whose rise has just annihilated his power. He has already poisoned the old King Ninus in the hope of securing the sceptre, and he is contemplating the assassination of the newly chosen king. At the moment of entering the tomb of the Assyrian monarch, where he hopes to take his victim by surprise, he suddenly experiences a mysterious uneasiness; his imagination presents to him some frightening phantoms.

The desire for vengence, anger, profound terror, bewilderment, the fear of death, supplication, such is the series of different shades with which this impassioned scene is stamped by turns.

When different but lightly distinct feelings succeed each other, the student should not only characterize them, but he should also space them so-to-say, in order that too much hurry does not cause one effect to destroy another and confuse the impressions of his listeners.

Rossini: *Semiramide*, Scene and Aria for basso.

Astonishment. Long and sustained.
As though fascinated. Slow.
Sombre timbre, ringing.
Distraught. Pursuing.
Round.
Clear timbre.
forte.
Cry of terror. Slow.
dès_so oh! quai sguar_di! un brando ei strin_ge s'avventa a mè fug_gia_mo ah! ch'ei m'ar.
Despair.
Painful supplication.
Clear timbre, ringing.
Round timbre.
Round timbre, ringing.
Dull, sombre timbre: concentrated.
Choking, affected voice.
Urging.
_res_ta la_sciami il crin m'af_fer_ra! d'un pie sfonda la ter_ra l'a_bis_so ei me l'ad_di_ta ei mi vi
This passage very slow although written in 16th and 32nd notes. The c[1] of the gruppetto very sustained.
Gradually anguished.
Distracted. Round, clear timbre
Slow.
Stressed.
Round, clear timbre.
Long.
Pleading. Dull, sombre timbre.
Sombre timbre, ringing.
spinge ah! nò Ciel ne poss' i_o da lui fuggir co_me sal_var_mi? oh Di_o!
All.º agitato.
Dull, sombre timbre.
Sombre timbre, ringing.
cresc.
Dull, sombre timbre.
forte
Dull, clear timbre.
piano
Deh ti ferma ti pla_ca per_do_na togli a me quell'or_ri bile as_pet_to quell' ac_
Assur.
Oppressed. The voice broken by exhalations.
Exhale.
Exhale.
Exhale.
Sombre timbre, ringing.
breath.
forte
Dull, sombre timbre. The voice extended.
Sombre timbre, ringing.
Inhale after the portamento.
piano
Dull, sombre timbre.
_cia_ro già sen_to nel pet_to quell'a_bis_so mi col_ma d'or_ror al_la pa_ce dell'om_bre ri_

Sombre timbre, ringing.
Dull, sombre timbre.
Accent displaced by syncopation.
Sombre timbre, ringing.
rinf.
tor - na ah pie_tà dell'oppresso mio cor ah pie_tà ah pie_tà ah pie_tà dell' op_pres_so mio
tor - - na ah pie_ta dell' oppres_so mio cor ah pia_ta ah pie_ta ah pie_ta dell' oppres - so mio
Dull, sombre timbre.
piano.
Sombre timbre, ringing.
forte.
Dull, sombre timbre.
piano.
piano. crescendo.
Breath.
cor deh ti ferma ah! ti placa ei mi_naccia deh per_do_na togli a me quell'or_ri_bil as_
cor deh ti ferma ah! ti pla_ca ei mi_naccia deh per_do_na togli a me quell' or_ri bile as_
Tone sustained with inflections.
Sombre timbre, ringing.
piano. rinforz.
forte. piano.
Dull, sombre timbre.
Sombre timbre, ringing.
mf
Exhalation.
Dull, sombre timbre.
dimin.
mez. forte.
piano.
_pet - - - to al_la pa_ce dell'ombra ri_tor - na ah! pie_tà dell' oppresso mio cor pietà pietà
_pet - - to al_la pa_ce dell'om_bra ri_tor - - na ah! pie_ta dell' op_presso mio cor pieta pieta
cresc.
sf piano.
piano.
forte.
cresc.
dell' op_presso oppres_so mio cor pietà pietà dell' op_
dell' op_preso oppres_so mi cor pieta pieta dell' op
Very equal and connected.
sf piano.
f
_pres_so oppres_so mio cor pie_tà ah pie_tà.
_pres_so op_pres_so mio cor pie_ta pie - - - - - - ta
pp

APPENDICES

APPENDIX I

VARIATIONS IN THE EDITION OF 1872

CHAPTER I

[A] Part Two opened with the following two paragraphs instead of the one given in 1847: In the first part of this work, we have recognized that the mechanism of singing includes four distinct apparatuses:

1. The lungs, bellows;
2. The larynx, vibrator;
3. The pharynx, reflector;
4. The organs of the mouth, articulators.

We studied the phenomena connected to the first three mechanisms at the same time, the emission of the voice and vocalization; now, by adding the fourth mechanism to the three others, we are going to concern ourselves with the result of that joining, that-is-to-say with singing properly so-called, or with the words joined to the music.

[B] Words, phrases, sentences, or paragraphs enclosed by asterisks (* . . . *) are omitted in the 1872 edition. If an entire footnote is omitted, the initial asterisk will precede the number; if any part of the footnote is retained, the initial asterisk will follow the number.

[C] The final sentence in this paragraph reads: One could however admit at least nine of them, for in the high notes of the two registers, one cannot do without the French vowels [ə] and [y].

[D] This example is replaced by "Che farò senza Euridice?" from

Orphée, by Gluck.

[E] The two paragraphs between the letters [E] are treated as part of a footnote to the preceding paragraph. The third paragraph of that footnote is the same as the first paragraph of footnote seven of the 1847 edition. The remainder of footnote seven is omitted.

[F] Footnote eleven is treated as regular text, inserted after the second appearance of the [F] on page fifteen.

[G] The table of consonant families follows the text of footnote eleven as it appears in the main text of 1872 (see note [F] above).

[H] Instead of *tanti*, the example *questo* [kwessəto] for [kwesto] is used. *Dunque* and *giorno* are not replaced.

[I] Although footnote twelve is omitted, Garcia adds the words *malgré* and *parfaitement* from Bérard's list, along with *lampo* [laməpo] for [lampo], and *mesta* [mɛsəta] for [mɛsta], to this list of examples of weak syllabication.

[J] The entire section between the letters [J] is omitted, as is footnote fourteen. The following sentence replaces all of the omitted material: When the consonants [m] or [n] end syllables in Italian singing, they require a special vigor to be heard clearly.

The indication for footnote thirteen follows that sentence.

[K] The 1872 edition lists the accents without the short paragraphs of explanation.

[L] All four examples following are omitted.

[M] Garcia inserts a comma and the word "abrupt" [*brusque*] here.

[N] This sentence reads: If at the moment of articulating

certain consonants or of vocalizing certain passages on these high notes, one neglects to support [*soutenir*] the exhalation, the glottis, forced naturally to contract in order to produce these high notes, closes completely, and the voice stops suddenly to reappear an instant later with an exaggerated or ridiculous explosion.

O The word "articulation" is substituted for the word "preparation" in this sentence.

P This sentence is changed to read: The voice is thus prolonged through the standing [*permanentes*] consonants without suffering the slightest interruption.

Q The word *e...glino* is added to this list of examples of [l].

R Footnote twenty-seven is interpolated into the text at this point, and the next two sentences are treated as two separate paragraphs.

S This sentence is expanded to read: The consonant should be pronounced only at the end of the syllable and of the tone, whatever the duration of it may be.

Also, the following example is added to that from Rossini's *Otello:*

Donizetti: *Lucia*, Final aria.

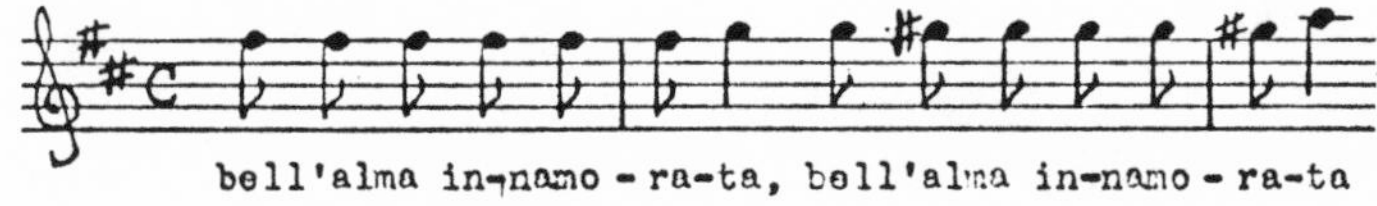
bell'alma in-namo - ra-ta, bell'alma in-namo - ra-ta

T The following material is inserted at this point: The explosive consonants completely stop the voice during their preparation.

Example: [See Arnold's exclamation, "Mon père, tu m'a du maudire!" from Rossini's *Guillaume Tell*, on page twenty-five.]

In order to obtain the breadth of the voice on the words, I have students declaim [*débiter*] several lines on the same pitch in the style of plainsong.

Entra l'uomo allor che nasce

In un mar di tante pene

Che s'avvezza dalle fasce

Ogni affanno a sostener, etc.

Metastasio: *Il sacrifizio d'Abramo*, Oratorio.

[U] This paragraph reads: The distribution of the words under the music should be done in such a manner that they mark the time [*mesure*] with regularity. One succeeds in it by making the common accent[84] fall on the first beat of the second, third or fourth measure, according to the length which the phrase or the member of the phrase presents relative to the verse. The reason for this is that these first beats mark the limit of the member of the phrase or of the melodic line. Only the meeting of this first beat with the common accent can indicate the rhythmic cadence. [The examples from *La Nozze di Figaro* and *Joseph* follow this abbreviated paragraph.]

[V] This sentence reads: In order to observe this precept, it is necessary to have in mind the laws of the formation of the musical phrase, those of the prosody of the language in which one is singing,

[84]The common accent is that which falls on the penultimate syllable of the smooth [*piano*] line of verse.

and those of its versification.[85]

[Another paragraph is added as follows.] In performance, one applies one syllable to each note, or to a group of notes slurred or barred together. When each syllable corresponds to a single note, the notes are written separately; when each syllable corresponds to a group of notes, the notes are joined by one or several bars, if their value permits, or by a slur if their value does not permit barring; in this latter case each group represents only the span [*place*] of one syllable.

W This paragraph reads: It happens very frequently in Italian singing that the number of notes [*places*] is less than that of the syllables to be placed. This takes place when different vowels are joined in succession [*se rencontrent*]; it is necessary then to contract them.

X Only the examples from the *Nozze* and *Sonnambula* are retained for the 1872 version, but the two examples below are added. The examples of the various combinations of two, three or four vowels are not presented separately, but are marked as they occur in the examples. The positions of the accents are not given either.

Rossini:
Semiramide,
Cavatina.
di gio-ja, di gio-ja e a-mor
Mozart:
Nozze di Figaro,
Aria.
fin chè l'aria è ancor bru-na e il mon-do ta-ce

---

[85]See pages 50-57, chap. II; and Scoppa, *Traité de versification*.

[Y] The romance from *Otello* as printed near the top of page forty-one and the cavatina from *Semiramide* as printed at the end of that same group of examples are used at this point as examples of elision.

[Z] The excerpt from *Don Giovanni* is used as an example of rule one. That from *Il Barbiere* is used to exemplify both rule two and rule three. The examples from *Cenerentola* and *Donna del lago* which appear below in the text are cited as further examples of avoiding the articulation of syllables on high notes.

[AA] Rules four and five are combined into a single sentence as follows: In order to avoid syllabication on a high note, one can either have recourse to a little lower note conveniently placed before the syllable, or else to a portamento.

The example from *Lucia* is used, but without the version illustrating the portamento.

CHAPTER II

[A] The initial heading of chapter two is THE MUSICAL PHRASE [*De la phrase musicale*].

[B] Footnote thirty-six is used here as a regular paragraph.

[C] In addition to the two examples given, Garcia adds Edgardo's aria, "Fra poco a me ricovero," from *Lucia*, which appears two paragraphs later in the 1847 edition. The sentence beginning after the second letter [C] appears after the three examples.

[D] The sixth edition gives only the version of the example from *Gazza ladra* with the suggested alterations.

[E] The word "accent" is substituted for "inflection."

[F] Instead of giving a separate example at this point, the reader is referred to the prior page (page seventy-one in this volume), to the aria "Fra poco a me ricovero," from *Lucia*, as an example of mixed time.

[G] The last sentence of this paragraph reads: One thus commits a grave fault, when, in order to render warmly the final cadences of pieces, one suddenly uses the ritardando in the next-to-the-last measure in place of the tempo rubato.

[H] The indication for footnote forty-five is given here.

[I] This measure is given as: 

[J] The first sentence of this paragraph reads: The portamento placed between two notes, of which each has its own particular syllable, is performed by leading the syllable which one is going to leave, and not as it is too often done in France, with the following syllable taken by anticipation.

[K] The aria of the Queen of the Night from *The Magic Flute* is added to that of Donna Anna from *Don Giovanni*:

The *Magic Flute* excerpt is followed by the following disclaimer: We cite this passage without daring to propose it for study.

[L] The example from *Semiramide* is placed here, and the next sentence begins a new paragraph.

M The following example is added here:

Zingarelli: *Romeo e Giulietta*, Aria.

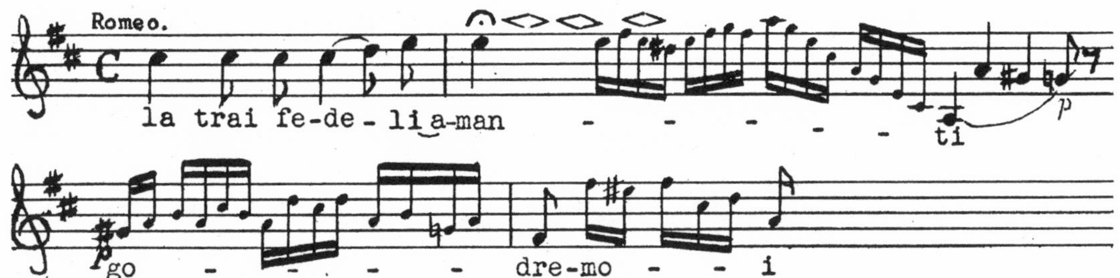
Romeo.
la trai fe-de-li a-man - - - - - ti
go - - - - - dre-mo - - i
p
Suspend and resume at the same dynamic level, and in the same timbre as before.

N In the 1872 edition, this sentence seems to refer to the Zingarelli example shown above. It reads: In this phrase, one should slow down, soften, and gradually carry the voice up to the first note of the motive.

O The Donizetti example is a major third higher in the 1872 edition (written in A Major).

CHAPTER III

A A footnote given here says: See *The Formation of the Phrase*.

B The word *chimère* is added to the list of French words.

C This first sentence is expanded to read: The appoggiatura, as its name indicates, is a note on which the voice marks a stress, and to which it accords in addition a prolongation of value more noticeable than on the resolving note.

D This sentence reads: The harmonists consider as appoggiaturas only the non-harmonic major and minor seconds attacked by conjunct intervals, but singers should, I believe, in addition to the seconds, count as appoggiaturas or at least subject to the same rules all the intervals which fulfill the same function, such as the delayed notes [*retards*] and the disjunct intervals.

E This sentence is added as a separate paragraph: The passage from the appoggiatura to the following note takes place with clarity [*limpidité*] by connecting the voice without drawling [*traîner*] it.

F This paragraph is expanded: The duration of the appoggiatura is quite variable. If the measure is even [*paire*], the appoggiatura is allotted one half of the note which is ornamented by it. If the original note is dotted, or if the measure is uneven [*impaire*], the appoggiatura borrows two thirds of its value. Finally the appoggiatura can be extremely [*excessivement*] rapid. The nature of the melody will determine the choice of these different applications more surely than rules [*préceptes*] could do.

G The reader is referred specifically to the section in Part One called *Battute di gola*, which is a small section under the broader one called *Little Notes*.

H The example from *Bianca e Faliero* is notated as follows:

I The order of this paragraph and the one following is reversed.

J The following example of syllabic organ point is the only one given in the 1872 edition.

Meyerbeer: *L'étoile du Nord*, Cadenza.

re-viens et j'a-ban-don-ne le scep-tre et la gran-deur! des-tin prends ma cou-
6
ron-ne, mais rends moi le bon-heur le bon-heur

CHAPTER IV

[A] Footnote fifty-seven is added to the paragraph, with only the source of the quote used as the footnote.

[B] Instead of the preceding two paragraphs, the 1872 edition has this one: We have said above (Part One, chapter VI [referring to the 1872 edition of Part One]) that each tone could receive the clear timbre or the sombre timbre, and that each timbre could, according to the taste of the singer, become brilliant or dull. These characteristics, offering very numerous combinations, permit the student to appropriately vary the expression of the voice. [The indication for footnote sixty-three is given at the end of this paragraph.]

[C] This sentence ends with the phrase: . . . but with a *more sombre* shade of the same timbre [translator's italics]. [Translator's note: The 1872 version is undoubtedly correct, as it is generally accepted that the timbres tend to be less differentiated in the male falsetto (middle) register. Indeed, the differentiation tends to lessen already in the passaggio tones of the male voices. In the female voices the same tones are affected in the same way, rather than the tones one octave higher in their passaggio into the head register.]

[D] The beginning: "The fragment of recitative . . . is divided into two effects," leads directly into the analysis of Desdemona's recitative. It is that example which appears in the space indicated by the ellipsis.

CHAPTER V

[A] After this abbreviated example, the following sentence and example are added: It would be more exact to write recitative by indicating the intervals, but without indicating the values. Example: Mozart: *Nozze di Figaro*, Recitative.

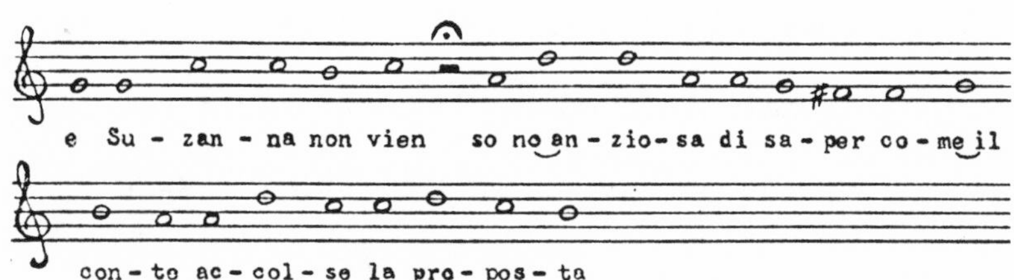
e Su - zan - na non vien so no an - zio - sa di sa - per co - me il
con - to ac - col - se la pro - pos - ta

[B] The sharp signs in parentheses in the following example were added in the 1872 edition.

[C] Garcia adds here: We have designated these notes by the sign + .

[D] The indication for footnote sixty-nine is given here.

[E] This paragraph is worded: The need for gradation is made so imperatively felt in this style that one cannot attack the *phrases* abruptly without offending the ear; those *phrases* which require the most boldness should be given out with an intensification [translator's italics]. The same observation is applied to isolated words.

[F] Footnotes seventy-one and seventy-two are inserted at the points of their indications as regular text material.

[G] The two soprano arias below are added to the list:

"La donna ha bello il core." Martini.

"La placida compagna." Pucitta.

APPENDIX II

TRANSLATOR'S NOTES

CHAPTER I

a) The reader is reminded that the table given on pages seven and eight is intended to indicate the pattern of modification while *ascending* in pitch. It corresponds to the progression of vowel changes taught to men singers today by many teachers. It would be interesting to hear a recording of one of the author's women students to see whether he actually used the same pattern with both sexes.

b) The pattern given for the clarification of the vowels, it will be noted, is the one commonly used for men's voices when *descending* in pitch.

c) Modern research and clinical observation indicate that whispering is very damaging to voices. Luchsinger and Arnold make particular mention of this fact in their book, *Voice-Speech-Language* (Belmont, California: Wadsworth Publishing Company, Inc., 1965), p. 120.

d) While Garcia states that this procedure of ending the syllables with the consonants is not the one to follow in singing songs, experience indicates that English speaking people often can obtain the necessary flow in singing Italian or French only by such a stratagem.

e) The following list of pieces was treated as a footnote in both editions. We felt that it was of sufficient importance to the development of the techniques under discussion to include it in the main text.

f) We cannot recall having seen an explanation of the rhythmic structure of Italian verse in any other book on singing. Although the author thought it possible to delete it from the 1872 edition, we felt it to be of sufficient value to move it from the position of a footnote to that of the regular text.

APPENDIX III

A CHRONOLIGICAL BIBLIOGRAPHY OF WORKS

BY MANUEL GARCIA

Mémoire sur la voix humaine, submitted to the French Academy of Sciences in 1840. Paris: E. Duverger, 1847.

The *Memoire* was Garcia's first formulation of the theories which he had developed from his work in the military hospital and his first ten years of experience as a teacher.

École de Garcia; Traité complet de l'Art du Chant. Paris: the author, 1840.

This publication contained only Part I.

École de Garcia; Traité complet de l'Art du Chant. Paris: the author, 1847.

Part I appears here in its second edition, Part II in its first edition. The two parts seem to have been available together or separately. This version appeared again in 1851 as the third edition.

École de Garcia; Traité complet de l'Art du Chant. Mayence: B. Schott's Sons, 1847.

Part I and Part II are in separate volumes and with separate pagination. The plate number of Part I indicates publication sometime during 1841, rather than 1847 as indicated on the Library of Congress card. The preface of Part I includes a lengthy extract from the *Memoire*. Both parts have parallel French and German texts.

Observations physiologiques sur la voix humaine. A translation of a memoire published in the "Proceedings of the Royal Society," vol. VII, no. 13. Paris: Masson, 1855.

These observations were made by the author following his invention of the laryngoscope in 1854. There was also a Spanish translation published in Madrid, but there seems to have been no English publication outside of the "Proceedings" until the magazine *Laryngoscope* reprinted it on the occasion of Garcia's hundredth birthday in 1905.

Nouveau Traité sommaire de l'Art du Chant. Paris: M. Richard, 1856.

The author referred to this as the fourth edition of his method. It was considerably abridged from the earlier editions, and it reflects some very slight alterations as a result of his use of the laryngoscope. This version continued to be reprinted throughout the author's lifetime, with the most recent which we found appearing in 1901 as the eleventh edition.

Hints on Singing. Trans. Beata Garcia. London: Ascherberg, Hopwood and Crew; New York: E. Schuberth and Company, 1894.
Garcia undertook this publication to clarify some misconceptions and to answer some criticisms of his method. It was written in question and answer form. His friend and former student, Hermann Klein, published an edition with minor revisions of terminology in 1911.

English Translations

Garcia's Complete School of Singing. London: Cramer, n.d.
No translator is indicated. It is apparently a condensation similar to the Albert Garcia translation below.

The Art of Singing, Part I. Boston: Oliver Ditson Company [18--?], n.d.
This is a nearly direct translation of the 1856 text. Ditson never published Part II. Theodore Presser Company reprinted this version in the 1940's. It is again out of print.

Garcia's Treatise on the Art of Singing. Ed. Albert Garcia. London: Leonard and Company, 1924.
This is essentially a translation of the 1856 version. The editor (a grandson of the author) further abridged the work and replaced some of the musical examples with those used in the earlier editions.